Psalm 91 by Peggy Joyce Ruth is a special book! I have shared it with many Christians and pastors, and it has become a very powerful and timely blessing for them and others. After reading it, they felt it was divinely inspired and opened powered truths of God's Word for our days and times. They quickly wanted more copies to share with their friends, pastors, and families. After reading the book, I was so impressed I contacted the author in Brownwood, Texas, to order cases to give away to those whom I felt really needed it. The author unlocks the mysteries of this psalm and shares many miraculous real-life miracles that have surrounded those who pray it in times of need.

—Robert Mills
Kitchener, Canada

This book, *Psalm 91*, has become one of my all-time favorites. It's an awesome book, and I have purchased many copies to share with friends and family. Thank you so much for writing it. Glory to God for giving us this amazing scripture and for giving you the ability, tools, and drive to complete it! Praise God, and thank you!

—Julie Schneider

Thank you for your work and all that I have learned from it. I came across your book *Psalm 91* at HEB and couldn't put it down once I started reading. I bought more copies for family members and have sent out a version of your *Psalm 91 Covenant* for them to pray daily, as I pray daily also. I have purchased additional copies for friends and family, and I am encouraging everyone to confess that prayer. It is now part of my daily regimen.

—John Schmit
Bryan, TX

Truly, mere words can't even begin to describe the gift that your book, *Psalm 91*, has been for me. In my own life it has probably made the difference between life and death. And, for the many others I have shared it with, well…all I can say is that it touches everyone who reads it.

My pain led me to search frantically in the Bible for answers, like in the Book of Psalms. I have known about the psalms all my life, but almost overnight the psalms became my best friends. I couldn't believe how accurately some of the psalms reflected my pain.

So, that was my state of mind one day as I was walking through Wal-Mart and saw your book. I had been reading the psalms a lot at that time, and your book just jumped right off the shelves at me—*Psalm 91*. I thought, "Why would anybody write a whole book about Psalm 91?" I started to pick it up and then thought, "No, this is crazy. There's nothing magical about Psalm 91. What could the book be about, anyway?" I walked away, almost laughing at myself. But then as I shopped, I kept thinking about that book: "Why would anyone write a whole book about a single psalm?" I returned to the bookshelf and took a look at it. *Psalm 91*—in a bright red cover, almost like blood. Hmmmm. "I think I'll get it." And I started to walk away with the book in my hand. But then I thought, "This is silly. Why am I so attracted to it? It is only a book—how good could it be, anyway?" So I walked back to the shelf and replaced it. And I walked away again. But once more, I felt called to that book! So I went back for a third time, thinking, "I've got to know what is so special about Psalm 91!" So I picked it up again, and this time I bought it and took it home with me.

Wow! This book was meant for me. Right then. Right now. This book was meant for me, and for all my family and friends too. It is powerful. And it *explains* things. It is about a psalm that is an incredible promise of protection from God, and the author painstakingly explains it throughout the chapters. "Wow!" is all I could think every time I read it. I was fascinated by it. I read it from cover to cover, and then read it again— outlining it as I read this time. Could this be real? I looked it up in the Bible, and sure enough, it was there, in *my* Bible. Now…*my* psalm. I began praying it over and over and over.

I was asked to give a devotion to my ladies group, and I gave it on the Ninety-first Psalm, with your book as my guide. I taught it to my kiddos at a youth group I started last fall. This book has been my lifeblood. I can't tell you the countless times I have prayed this psalm and received God's protection.

I am an attorney. I give my attorney associates copies of your book. Some of them take two or three copies because they want one for their mom or their sister, a brother, or a friend. I share with as many friends and associates as I can. I've never had anyone turn my offer of a book down. Literally everyone I have shared your book with ended up sharing it with someone else because it was so meaningful to them.

Your book, *Psalm 91*, is awesome! God bless you, and thank you so much for believing in our Lord Jesus Christ enough to take the time out of your life to write this awesome book. I will forever treasure it and the work I have seen it do in my life and in the lives of so many of my friends, family, clients, and all the folks they have given it to as well. Thank you, Mrs. Ruth. *Thank you.*

—ATTORNEY JACKIE BARROW
MISSOURI

I came across a book entitled *Psalm 91: God's Shield of Protection*. Since I've always loved that particular psalm, I decided to buy the book. I have read and reread that book a number of times. The pages are marked with comments written by me of things that God had placed in my heart as I read the book. I have never read Psalm 91 with such incredible revelation. I can hardly put the book down. I finish reading the first twenty-one chapters, then I start it all over again. Every time I reread it, God reveals something new to me. Thank you so much! I'm so excited about this book, and I want to purchase it for a number of people. I will continue to reread this book and let the power of the Word wash over me. I appreciate you!

—CAROL BROSAM
ILLINOIS

PSALM 91

PEGGY JOYCE RUTH
ANGELIA RUTH SCHUM

CHARISMA
HOUSE

Library of Congress Cataloging-in-Publication Data

Ruth, Peggy Joyce.
  Psalm 91 / Peggy Joyce Ruth, Angelia Ruth Schum.
  p. cm.
  Includes bibliographical references.
  ISBN 978-1-63641-187-3
  1. Bible. O.T. Psalm XCI--Criticism, interpretation, etc. 2.
Christian biography. I. Schum, Angelia Ruth. II. Title.
  BS145091st .R87 2010
  223'.206--dc22
                        2010012356

E-book ISBN: 978-1-61638-398-5

20 21 22 23 24 — 23 22 21 20 19

CONTENTS

SECTION I: PSALM 91

SECTION II: STORIES THAT DEMAND TO BE TOLD—PSALM 91 TESTIMONIES

CONTENTS

SECTION III: A PRAYER COVENANT

FOREWORD

GENERAL GEORGE C. MARSHALL, U.S. Army Chief of Staff during World War II, once said, "We are building... morale, not on supreme confidence in our ability to conquer and subdue other peoples, not in reliance on things of steel and the super-excellence of guns and planes and bombsights... [but] on things more potent. We are building it on *belief;* for it is what men believe that makes them invincible."[1]

During my experience as a chaplain to a battalion of U.S. Marines in Iraq, I saw firsthand what happens when *belief in Almighty God* floods the hearts and souls of men and women rushing into battle. This supreme confidence in God is not *foxhole religion or superficial faith.* It is a life-changing decision to place oneself in the loving hands of Him who is greater than the battlefield.

Such a faith is nowhere more vividly demonstrated than in the words of Psalm 91. For thousands of years the "Soldier's Psalm" has given warriors a reservoir of truth to draw from when the night is dark and the task is difficult. In this timely companion to this timeless psalm, Peggy Joyce Ruth has made clear and accessible the power of God's promises to those who face the ruination and rubble of war.

For those on the home front, read this book as a practical guide to radical intercessory prayer on behalf of your marine, sailor, soldier, or airman.

For those heroes on the front lines, read this book for strength, hope, courage, and salvation. And as you walk with God through the valley of the shadow of death, may the awesome power of His promises, shared in this book, fill your heart, rule your mind, and shield your life. For, "He who dwells in the shelter of the Most High will abide in the shadow of the Almighty" (Ps. 91:1).

—LIEUTENANT CAREY H. CASH, CHAPLAIN, USN

Author's Note:

Lieutenant Carey H. Cash has been a battalion chaplain to infantry marines. He is currently chaplain to the president at Camp David. In Operation Iraqi Freedom, his unit was the first ground combat force to cross the border into Iraq. He is a graduate of The Citadel and Southwestern Baptist Theological Seminary and was commissioned as a chaplain in 1999.

In his book, *A Table in the Presence*, he relates the stories from the men with whom he was privileged to serve. In one of these stories, he says: "Early on April 12, as I made my way around Saddam's palace grounds, I felt compelled to keep talking to the men and listening to their stories. I sensed in them a deep need, even a compulsion, to artic- ulate their wonder and amazement at what God had brought them through. And this wasn't true of only a handful of Marines. From the youngest private to the oldest veteran, every man seemed to have a story to tell.... Their stories seemed to have one common thread—they all believed they had been in the midst of a modern-day miracle. As they told me what they had seen, their eyes lit up, and their faces glowed. It was clear to me that I wasn't merely in the company of warriors, but of witnesses.... As they spoke, with tears in their eyes and bullet holes through their clothes, I realized that I too was a witness. These were not men who had 'found religion' momentarily, or who were courte- ously acknowledging the practical aspects of prayer or faith in times of need. These were men who had stumbled onto something historic... a story that had to be told."[2]

Psalm 91

He who dwells in the shelter of the Most High
Will abide in the shadow of the Almighty.
I will say to the LORD, "My refuge and my fortress,
My God, in whom I trust!"
For it is He who delivers you from the snare of the trapper
And from the deadly pestilence.
He will cover you with His pinions,
And under His wings you may seek refuge; His faithfulness is a
shield and bulwark.

You will not be afraid of the terror by night,
Or of the arrow that flies by day;
Of the pestilence that stalks in darkness,
Or of the destruction that lays waste at noon.
A thousand may fall at your side
And ten thousand at your right hand,
But it shall not approach you.
You will only look on with your eyes
And see the recompense of the wicked.
For you have made the LORD, my refuge,
Even the Most High, your dwelling place.
No evil will befall you,
Nor will any plague come near your tent.

For He will give His angels charge concerning you,
To guard you in all your ways.
They will bear you up in their hands,
That you do not strike your foot against a stone.
You will tread upon the lion and cobra,
The young lion and the serpent you will trample down.

"Because he has loved Me, therefore I will deliver him;
I will set him securely on high, because he has known My name.
"He will call upon Me, and I will answer him;
I will be with him in trouble;
I will rescue him and honor him.
"With a long life I will satisfy him
And let him see My salvation."

The Power of Psalm 91

When a Pennsylvania lieutenant was accidentally discovered by the enemy while attempting to carry out a
very important overseas mission, he immediately placed
himself in the hands of God, but all he could get out
of his mouth was, "Lord, it's up to You now." Before he
had a chance to defend himself, the enemy shot point-
blank, striking him in the chest and knocking him flat
on his back. Thinking he was dead, his buddy grabbed
the carbine out of his hands, paired it up with his own,
and began blasting away with both guns. When his
friend finished, not one enemy was left. Later, the lieutenant's sister in Pennsylvania got a letter relating this
amazing story. The force of that bullet in the chest had
only stunned her brother. Without thinking, he reached
for the wound, but instead he felt his Bible in his pocket.
Pulling it out, he found an ugly hole in the cover. The
Bible he carried had shielded his heart. The bullet had
ripped through Genesis, Exodus…and had kept going
through book after book, stopping in the middle of
the Ninety-first Psalm, pointing like a finger at verse 7:
"A thousand may fall at your side, and ten thousand at
your right hand; but it shall not come near you" (NKJV).
The lieutenant exclaimed, "I did not know such a verse
was in the Bible, but precious God, I thank You for it."[1]
He did not realize this protection psalm even existed
until the Lord supernaturally revealed it to him.

Perhaps your protection may not manifest itself as
dramatically as it did with this army lieutenant, but your
promise is just as reliable. This book will demonstrate
the power of Psalm 91 to *literally* save your life!

Introduction

SETTING the SCENE

S UNDAYS WERE USUALLY A comfort—but not on this particular
Sunday! Our pastor looked unusually serious that day as he made
the announcement that one of our most beloved and faithful dea-
cons had been diagnosed with leukemia and had only a few weeks to
live. Only the Sunday before, this robust-looking deacon in his mid-
forties had been in his regular place in the choir, looking as healthy
and happy as ever. Now, one Sunday later, the entire congregation was
in a state of shock after hearing such an unexpected announcement.
However, little did I know this incident would pave the way to a message that was going to forever burn in my heart.

Surprisingly, I had gone home from church that day feeling very
little fear, perhaps because I was numb from the shock of what I had
heard. I vividly remember sitting down on the edge of the bed that
afternoon and saying out loud: "Lord, is there any way to be protected
from all the evils that are coming on the earth?" I was not expecting an
answer; I was merely voicing the thought that kept replaying over and
over in my mind. I remember lying across the bed and falling immediately to sleep, only to wake up a short five minutes later. However, in
those five minutes I had a very unusual dream.

In the dream I was in an open field, asking the same question that I
had prayed earlier—"Is there any way to be protected from all the things
that are coming on the earth?" And in my dream, I heard these words:

In your day of trouble call upon Me, and I will answer you!

Suddenly, I knew I had the answer I had so long been searching for. The ecstatic joy I felt was beyond anything I could ever describe. To my surprise, instantly there were hundreds with me in the dream out in that open field, praising and thanking God for the answer. It wasn't until the next day, however, when I heard the Ninety-first Psalm referred to on a tape by Shirley Boone, that I suddenly *knew in my heart* that *whatever* was in that psalm was God's answer to my question. I nearly tore up my Bible in my haste to see what it said. There it was in verse 15—the *exact statement* God had spoken to me in my dream. I could hardly believe my eyes!

I believe that you who are reading this book are among the many Christians to whom God is supernaturally revealing this psalm. You were the ones pictured with me in my dream in that open field who will, through the message in this book, get your answer to the question, "Can a Christian be protected through these turbulent times?"

Since the early 1970s, I have had many opportunities to share this message. I feel God has commissioned me to write this book to proclaim God's *covenant of protection*. May you be sincerely blessed by it.

—Peggy Joyce Ruth

Section

PSALM 91

Chapter

1

WHERE IS MY DWELLING PLACE?

He who dwells in the shelter of the Most High
Will abide in the shadow of the Almighty.

—Psalm 91:1

Have you ever been inside a cabin with a big roaring fire in the fireplace, enjoying a wonderful feeling of safety and security as you watch an enormous electrical storm going on outside? It is a warm, wonderful sensation, knowing you are being sheltered and protected from the storm. That is what Psalm 91 is all about—*shelter*!

I am sure you can think of something that represents *security* to you personally. When I think of security and protection, I have a couple of childhood memories that automatically come to mind. My dad was a large, muscular man who played football during his high school and college years, but he interrupted his education to serve in the military during World War II. Mother, who was pregnant with my little brother, and I lived with my grandparents in San Saba, Texas, while Dad was in the service. As young as I was, I vividly remember one ecstatically happy day when my dad unexpectedly opened the door and walked into my grandmother's living room. Before that eventful day, I had been tormented with fears because some neighborhood children had told me I would never see my dad again. Like kids telling a ghost story, they taunted me that my dad would come home in a box. When he walked through that door, *a sense of peace and security came over me and stayed with me for the rest of his time in the army.*

It was past time for my baby brother to be born, and I found out when I was older that Dad's outfit at the time was being relocated by train from Long Beach, California, to Virginia Beach, Virginia. The train was coming through Fort Worth, Texas, on its way to Virginia, so my dad caught a ride from Fort Worth to San Saba in the hopes of seeing his new son. He then hitchhiked until he caught up with the train shortly before it reached Virginia Beach. The memory of his walking into that room still brings a feeling of peaceful calm to my soul. In fact, that incident set the stage for later seeking the security a *heavenly* Father's presence could bring.

Did you know there is a place in God—a secret place—for those who want to seek refuge? *It is a literal place of physical safety and security that God tells us about in Psalm 91.*

Dwelling in the shelter of the Most High is the Old Testament's way of teaching faith. This gives us the most intense illustration of the very essence of a personal relationship with God. Man has no innate built-in shelter. Alone, he stands unsheltered against the elements and must run to *the shelter* Himself. In the first verse of Psalm 91, God offers us more than protection; it is as if He rolls out the hospitality mat and personally invites us in.

I cannot talk about this kind of peace and security without also having another vivid memory come to mind. My parents once took my younger siblings and me fishing on a lake near Brownwood, Texas, for an afternoon of fun.

Dad had a secluded place where we fished for perch. That was the second greatest highlight of the outing. I loved seeing the cork begin to bob and then suddenly go completely out of sight. There were only a few things that could thrill me more than jerking back on that old, cane pole and landing a huge perch right in the boat. I think I was fully grown before I realized that Dad had an ulterior motive in taking us for an afternoon of perch fishing. He used the perch as bait for the trotline he had stretched out across one of the secret coves at the lake.

Dad would drive the boat over to the place where his trotline was located, cut off the boat motor, and inch the boat across the cove as he *ran the trotline.* That's what he called it when he took the trotline into his hands and pulled the boat alongside all the strategically placed, baited hooks to see if any of them had caught a large catfish.

I said that catching the perch was the *second* greatest highlight of the outing. By far the greatest thrill came when Dad would get to a place where the trotline would begin to jerk almost out of his hand. Then we three siblings would watch, wide-eyed, as Dad wrestled with the line until finally, in victory, he would flip a huge catfish over the side of the boat, right on the floorboard at our feet. Money couldn't buy that kind of excitement! Not even the circus and a carnival all rolled up into one could compete with that kind of a thrill.

However, one of these outings turned out to be more eventful than most, quickly becoming an experience I will never forget. It had been beautiful when we started out, but by the time we finished our perch fishing and headed toward the cove, everything had changed. A storm came upon the lake so suddenly there was no time to get back to the boat dock. The sky turned black, lightning flashed, and drops of rain fell with such force they actually stung when they hit. Moments later, we were being pelted by marble-sized hailstones.

I saw the fear in my mother's eyes, and I knew we were in danger. But before I had time to wonder what we were going to do, Dad had driven the boat to the rugged shoreline of the only island on the lake. Although boat docks surround the island now, back then it looked like an abandoned island with absolutely no place to take cover. Within

7

moments Dad had us all out of the boat and ordered the three of us to lie down beside our mother on the ground. He quickly pulled a canvas tarp out of the bottom of the boat, knelt down on the ground beside us, and thrust the tarp up over all five of us. That storm continued to rage outside the makeshift tent he had fashioned over us—the rain beat down, the lightning flashed, and the thunder rolled. Yet I could think of nothing else but how it felt to have my dad's arms around us. There was a certain calm under the protection of the shield my father had provided that is hard to explain now. In fact, I had never felt as safe and secure in my entire life. I remember thinking that I wished the storm would last forever. I didn't want anything to spoil the wonderful security I felt that day *in our secret hiding place*. Feeling my father's protective arms around me, I never wanted the moment to end.

Although I have never forgotten that experience, today it has taken on new meaning. Just as Dad put a tarp over us to shield us from the storm, our heavenly Father has a *secret place* in His arms that protects us from the storms that are raging in the world around us.

That *secret place* is literal, but it is also conditional! In verse 1 of Psalm 91, God lists our part of the condition before He even mentions the promises included in His part. That's because *our part* has to come first. To abide in the *shadow* of the Almighty, we must first *choose to dwell* in the shelter of the Most High.

The question is, "How do we dwell in the security and shelter of the Most High?" It is more than an intellectual experience. This verse speaks of a dwelling place in which we can be physically protected if we run to Him. You may utterly believe that God is your refuge, you may give mental assent to it in your prayer time, you may teach Sunday School lessons on this concept of refuge, and you may even get a warm feeling every time you think of it, but unless you do something about it—*unless you actually get up and run to the shelter*—you will never experience it.

You might call that place of refuge—a *love walk*! In fact, the secret place is, in reality, the intimacy and familiarity of the presence of God Himself. When our grandchildren Cullen, ten, and Meritt, seven, stay the night with us, the moment they finish breakfast each runs to his own secret place to spend some time talking with God. Cullen finds a place behind the couch in the den, and Meritt heads behind the lamp table in the corner of our bedroom. Those places have become very special to them.

Where is your secret place? You too need the security and shelter of a secret place with the Most High.

Chapter

2

WHAT IS COMING OUT OF MY MOUTH?

I will say to the LORD, "My refuge and my fortress,
My God, in whom I trust!"

—PSALM 91:2

NOTICE THAT VERSE 2 above says, "I will say..." Circle the word *say* in your Bible, because we must learn to verbalize our trust. We answer back to God what He says to us in the first verse. There is power in saying His Word back to Him!

We are not told simply to *think* the Word. We are told to *say* the Word. For example, Joel 3:10 tells the weak to say: "I am a mighty man." Over and over we find great men of God like David, Joshua, Shadrach, Meshach, and Abednego declaring their confessions of faith aloud in dangerous situations. Notice what begins to happen on the inside when you say, "Lord, You are my refuge—You are my fortress—You are my

11

Lord and my God! It is in You that I put my total trust!" The more we say it aloud, the more confident we become in His protection.

So many times, as Christians, we mentally agree that the Lord is our refuge—but that is not enough. Power is released in saying it out loud. When we say it and mean it, we are placing ourselves in His shelter. By voicing His lordship and His protection, we open the door to the secret place.

One cannot miss the fact that this verse uses the word *my* three times: "my refuge," "my fortress," "my God"! The psalmist makes a personal claim to God. The reason we can trust is that we know who God is to us. This verse makes the analogy of who God is; He is a *refuge* and a *fortress*. These metaphors are significant military terms. God Himself becomes the defensive site for us against all invading enemies. He is personally our protection.

Have you ever tried to protect yourself from all the bad things that can happen? God knows we can't do it. Psalm 60:11 tells us: "...deliverance by man is in vain." God has to be our refuge before the promises in Psalm 91 will ever work.

We can go to the doctor once a month for a checkup. We can double-check our cars every day to make sure the motors, the tires, and the brakes are all in good working order. We can fireproof our houses, and we can store up food for a time when we may be in need. We can take every precaution imaginable that the military offers, yet we still cannot do enough to protect ourselves from every potential danger life has to offer. It's impossible!

It isn't that any one of these precautions is wrong. It is that not one of these things, in and of itself, has the power to protect. God has to be the one to whom we run first. *He is the only one who has an answer for whatever might come.*

When I think of how utterly impossible it is to protect ourselves from all the evils in the world, I am reminded of sheep. Sheep have no real protection other than their shepherd. In fact, a sheep is the only animal I can think of that has *no* built-in protection. It has no sharp teeth, no offensive odor to spray to drive off its enemies, no loud bark, and it certainly can't run fast enough to escape danger. That's why the Bible calls us God's sheep! God is saying, "I want you to see Me as your source of protection. I am your shepherd." Now He may use doctors, policemen, firemen, storm cellars, bank accounts, and so forth to meet our specific needs, but our hearts have to run to Him first as our shepherd and our protector. Then *He* will choose the method He desires to bring about the protection.

Some quote Psalm 91 as though it was some kind of *magic wand*, but there is nothing magical about this psalm. It is powerful, and it works simply because it is the Word of God, alive and active. And we confess it aloud simply because the Bible tells us to do so.

When I'm facing a challenge, I have learned to say: "In this particular situation [name the situation aloud] I choose to trust You, Lord." The difference it makes when I proclaim my trust aloud is amazing.

Take notice of what flies out of your mouth in times of trouble. The worst thing that can happen is for something to come out that brings death. Cursing gives God nothing to work with. This psalm tells us to do just the opposite—speak life!

C. B. Morelock, a war correspondent in World War II, reported an unexplainable and miraculous occurrence: sixty German aircraft strafed more than four hundred men who were pinned down on the sandy Dunkirk beaches without the benefit of anyplace to take cover. Although the men were repeatedly attacked by machine guns and bombed by enemy aircraft, not one single man was hit. Every man *in that group* left the beach without a scratch. Morelock stated, "I have personally been told by Navy men who picked up those particular survivors from Dunkirk, that the men not only recited Psalm 91, *but they shouted it aloud at the top of their lungs!*"[1] Saying our trust out loud releases faith!

Another time when God brought life to a death situation stands out in my mind. The whole family was rejoicing when our daughter-in-law, Sloan, received a positive pregnancy test report and found she was going to have the first grandchild on either side of the family. Since she'd had a tubal pregnancy once before, making her highly susceptible for another, the doctor ordered a sonogram as a precautionary measure.

The disturbing result of the sonogram was: "no fetus found, a great deal of water in the uterus and spots of endometriosis." With only two hours' notice, emergency surgery was quickly underway, at which time the doctor performed a laparoscopy, drained the uterus, and scraped away the endometriosis. After the surgery the doctor's words were, "During the laparoscopy we carefully looked everywhere, and there was no sign of a baby, but I want to see you back in my office in one week to be sure fluid doesn't build back up." When Sloan argued that the pregnancy test had been positive, he said there was a 99 percent chance the baby had naturally aborted and had been absorbed into the uterine lining.

Even so, after the doctor left the room, Sloan was the only one not fazed by his report. What she said next surprised everyone. She emphatically stated that even the doctor had left her with a 1 percent chance, and she was going to take it. From that moment on, no amount of discouragement from well-meaning friends who didn't want her to be disappointed had any effect on her. Never once did she veer away from confessing out loud Psalm 91 and another Scripture promise that she had found: "[My child] will not die, but live, and tell of the works of the LORD" (Ps. 118:17). A treasured book that was very important to Sloan during this time was *Supernatural Childbirth* by Jackie Mize.[2]

A strange look came on the technician's face the next week as she administered the ultrasound. She immediately called for the physician. Her reaction was a little disconcerting to Sloan, until Sloan heard these words: "Doctor, I think you need to come here quickly. I've just found a six-week-old fetus!" It was nothing short of a miracle that such severe, invasive procedures had not damaged or destroyed this delicate life in its beginning stages. When I look at my grandson, it is hard to imagine life without him. I thank God for a daughter-in-law who believes in her covenant and is not ashamed *to confess it out loud* in the face of every negative report.

Our part of this protection covenant is expressed in verses 1 and 2 of Psalm 91. Note very carefully these words: "he who *dwells…*" and "I will *say…*" These words, which amount to *our responsibility* under the terms of this covenant, release God's power to fulfill His amazing promises, which are given to us in verses 3–16, which we will look at in the following chapters.

Chapter

3

TWO-WAY DELIVERANCE

For it is He who delivers you from the snare of the trapper and from the deadly pestilence.

—Psalm 91:3

HAVE YOU EVER SEEN a movie where a fur trapper travels deep into the mountains in the cold climate? He baits big, steel traps, covers them over with branches, and then waits for some unsuspecting animal to step into the trap. Those traps were not there by chance. The trapper has taken great care in placing them in very strategic locations. In times of war a minefield is set up the same way. Those land mines are methodically placed in well-calculated locations.

These are pictures of what the enemy does to us. That is why he is called the *trapper*! The traps that are set for us are not there by accident. It is as if the trap has your name on it. They are custom made, placed, and baited specifically for each one of us. But like an animal

17

caught in a trap, when ensnared, we suffer through a slow, painful process. We don't die instantly. We are ensnared until the trapper comes to destroy us.

I will never forget a tragedy that happened to a good friend of mine Her husband, having quit in the middle of numerous career possibilities requiring a number of expensive moves, finally joined the army without consulting anyone, including his wife. It was hard on this young wife who had faithfully undergone countless abrupt alterations and changes of direction in her way of life. However, she was very supportive and constantly defended her husband's behavior.

Unfortunately, his low self-esteem and immature conduct left him a prime candidate to fall into one of the enemy's traps. He had been so accustomed to giving in to his flesh that when the enemy placed a beautiful, willing young girl in front of him, he temporarily forgot the faithful young wife back home who had supported him through so much. That was the straw that *broke the camel's back*. It is not repetitive to say, "Hurting people hurt people." This couple got caught in a downward spiral. Her years of pain and self-sacrifice left her hopeless, and the marriage could never be restored. Because the couple was ignorant of the schemes of the enemy, the trap so carefully laid accomplished exactly what the trapper set out to accomplish. The bait was set at the exact moment this man was most vulnerable to fall.

The enemy knows exactly what will most likely hook us, and he knows exactly which *thought* to put into our minds to lure us into the trap. That is why Paul tells us in 2 Corinthians 2:11 that we are "not [to be] ignorant of his schemes." Then he says:

> For the weapons of our warfare are not of the flesh, but divinely powerful for the destruction of fortresses. We are destroying speculations and every lofty thing raised up against the knowledge of God, and we are taking every thought captive to the obedience of Christ.
>
> —2 Corinthians 10:4–5

God not only delivers us from the snare laid by the trapper (Satan), but according to the last part of Psalm 91:3, He also delivers us from the deadly *pestilence*. I always thought a pestilence was something that attacked crops—bugs, locusts, grasshoppers, spider mites, mildew, or root rot. After doing a word study on the word *pestilence*, however, I found, to my surprise, that pestilence attacks people—not crops!

Pestilence is "any virulent or fatal disease; an epidemic that hits the masses of people."[1] These deadly diseases attach themselves to a person's body with the intent to destroy it. But God tells us in verse 3 that He will deliver us from these deadly diseases.

There are all kinds of enemies: temptations, spiritual enemies, and physical enemies. Doctors who study germs and bacterial attacks against the body describe cellular battle scenes comparable to military conflicts. Not surprisingly, each of these enemies works in similar, strategic ways. Initially, I was in a quandary after my word study, wondering if God really meant literal pestilence. It took me awhile to see the spiritual side of enemy attacks and the internal workings of warfare in the body as a parallel concept with disease. Only man tries to choose between physical and spiritual deliverance; Scripture includes both. (Notice how Jesus demonstrates that His power operates at all levels with a very literal, physical fulfillment in Matthew 8:16–17.) When evil is served, it looks the same on the platter. Scripture deals with both through clear verses that promise physical healing and literal deliverance.

God is so good to confirm His Word when one seeks Him with an open heart. Right after I received the dream about Psalm 91 and was trying to digest all of these protection promises and comprehend the fact that God is the one who always sends good and not evil, Satan was on the other end trying to discourage my faith at every turn. Because I was very young in my conviction, and struggling hard to maintain it in the midst of a world that does not believe in the supernatural goodness of God, I was devastated when a thought came into my mind one morning as I was getting ready to go to church: "If God wants us to walk in health, why did He create germs?" That one thought was attempting to completely dismantle my faith in the newfound truth that God had provided healing in the atonement.

In fact, I was so distraught I didn't even think I could motivate myself to go to church that morning. I remember going into my bedroom where I literally fell on my face before God, asking Him how those two facts could possibly be reconciled. As clear as a bell, God spoke in my spirit: "Trust Me, get up and go, and I will give you an answer." I got up with mixed emotions. I had unmistakably heard God speak to my spirit, but I could see no way in which He could satisfactorily resolve that question that had stuck in my head. Why *would* God create a germ to make us sick, if He did in fact want us to walk in divine health? I went to church that morning under a cloud of heaviness, and I couldn't tell you what subject the pastor, Bert Maxfield, preached on. But somewhere in the middle of his sermon he made this statement: "God made everything good. Take germs, for instance—germs are nothing more than microscopic plants and animals that the enemy perverted and uses to spread disease." Then he stopped and, with a strange look on his face, said, "I have no idea where that thought came from. It was not in my notes." He went right on with his sermon. I must admit I almost disturbed the entire service because I couldn't keep from bouncing up and down on the pew. The awesomeness of God was more than I could take in without it erupting out of me. God could not have done anything that would have strengthened my faith for healing more than that incident did that morning.

Do you sometimes feel you have opposition facing you from every side? Psalm 91:3 addresses the enemy's assaults from both the physical and the spiritual. One of our family members went to a certain country as a missionary and made the comment, "This is a country where there are lots of ways to die." Both the poor health conditions and the hostility in the country provided many dangers. You will encounter enemies that attack your mind (thoughts), some that attack your body internally (germs), and some who attack with weapons (people). This is your verse, ensuring your deliverance from all the varieties of harm.

Consider with me one more area of physical protection from harm.

Often in war, traps are set that can toy with the human mind—tragedies in which innocent people are accidentally killed. I believe this is addressed in Scripture also. When Jesus sent the disciples out, He gave these instructions: "I send you out as sheep in the midst of wolves; so be shrewd as serpents and innocent as doves" (Matt. 10:16). It is an interesting instruction to be told to have the cleverness of a snake (so as not to be harmed) but the innocence of a dove (so as not to cause harm). Each year at the Texas Rattlesnake Roundup, men often disassemble rattlesnakes with their knives for the gaping audience. They pry open the snake's mouth to reveal the fangs and milk it of its poison. Then with a knife they slice open the thick, scaly skin covering with its agile muscular structure. After seeing the internal workings, it becomes obvious the snake is built for causing harm. Not so with the dove. When a hunter cleans a dove, first he pulls off the feathers. There are no thick scales, no dangerous claws, no poisonous venom. The dove has nothing in it that causes harm. In this analogy, we are advised as sheep among wolves to be as clever as the snake but as innocent as the dove. This takes care of harm in two directions. I believe we are to claim the promise of this verse—for God to protect us from being harmed and from harming innocent people. Pray, for example, that God protects you from ever hitting a child on a bicycle, being involved in a wreck that kills another person, or causing someone to walk away from the faith.

Many a person has been traumatized from inadvertently hurting someone he never intended to hurt. In the military, a soldier's conscience can be easily wounded by causing unintended harm such as accidental friendly fire, a medic's mistake on a patient, a plan that backfires, or a civilian killed by a stray bullet. Just like a soldier, we need to be delivered from unintentional harm as well.

God put this preventive promise in verse 3 for you to stand on for protection from both ways in which harm can destroy a life.

It would be shocking to actually realize how often Satan has a set trap just waiting for us. How devastating the results can be! My daughter was using an animal trap as an illustration in her Bible study. She had actually set the trap and as an extra precaution had a student guarding it so no one would be accidentally hurt. However, somehow one of the more impulsive students, in a split second, walked up and simply put his thumb on the most treacherous part of the trap, asking, "What's this?" It snapped shut. It looked like the thumb might have been severed, and it took two people on each side of the trap to get his thumb out. Since the teaching was being recorded, you could hear the screams, the slamming of the trap's hinge, and the hysteria of those trying to help get the trap open.

The hurt student said his pain would not have been so bad if one of those *helping* had not tried to take his thumb out before the trap was opened. Some of you, like that student who put his finger in the trap, need to train yourself to stop during the split second when temptation rears its ugly head. Say out loud: "God delivers me from the snare of *the trapper*—that thing that makes me lose my temper, that lust that tries to rise up in my heart, that person who constantly offends me, that wrong thing that comes flying out of my mouth in a heated moment, and that situation that always causes me to get frustrated."

I don't know too many people who have thought of Psalm 91 as a good scriptural promise to help out in temptation and to keep someone from getting caught in that trap of repetitive sin. Verse 3 is a good promise for deliverance to get in your heart and have coming out your mouth as protection from traps that can actually destroy your life! Just as you can't imagine why someone would put his finger in a trap to test it, Psalm 91 has a provision for those impulsive sins that we do without thinking.

This is a powerful verse that speaks of more than just one kind of trap. Pay special attention to the twofold aspect to this deliverance: (1) from the *snare of the trapper*, and (2) from the *deadly pestilence*. This covers being delivered from temptation and being delivered from harm. It is similar to the request in the Lord's Prayer: "Do not lead us into temptation, but deliver us from evil" (Matt. 6:13).

Our son, Bill, was born with a serious membrane disease in his lungs. We were alarmed because it was the same disease that had killed

President Kennedy's baby, even with some of the best doctors, just a short time before Bill was born.

None of the hospital staff expected Bill to live, and he was placed in an incubator for over a month. Every day we would go to the hospital just to watch him through a huge glass window. It was a hard time, but somehow God gave my husband and me a gift of faith to believe he would live and not die.

It is so amazing to see all the different ways in which God works mysteriously when you are trusting in His Word. Our little hometown doctor was definitely sent by God. Two of his nephews had died from that same disease, and he had quit practicing medicine for a while to study and try to find a cure for it. In fact, the doctor had only recently returned to practicing medicine when Bill was born. So when he discovered that Bill had the exact same disease his nephews had, he started trying everything on Bill he had read about during his studies. And miraculously, Bill started responding to one of the methods. Thanks be to God for this promise—for it is He who delivers us from the deadly pestilence. Instead of losing our baby, we were able to bring home a perfectly healed, healthy baby boy from the hospital. Whatever you are believing for…whatever you are going though…Psalm 91 speaks to the protection available to us from all the fatal diseases that are in the world around us.

What good would it do to be delivered from harm only to be caught in a sin that destroys us? On the other hand, what good would it do to be delivered from a sin only to be destroyed by a deadly pestilence? This verse covers both. Thank God for His deliverance from both traps and pestilence.

Chapter

UNDER HIS WINGS

He will cover you with His pinions,
And under His wings you may seek refuge.
—PSALM 91:4

WHEN YOU PICTURE A magnificent flying bird, it is usually not a chicken that comes to mind. I've never seen a chicken portrayed in flight—many eagles, but no chickens. We quote the scripture from Isaiah 40:31 that talks about being borne up on the wings of eagles or with wings like eagles. There is a difference, however, between being *on* His wings and being *under* His wings. This promise in Psalm 91 is not elaborating on the *flying* wing—but on the *sheltering* wing. One indicates *strength* and *accomplishment*, while the other denotes *protection* and *familiarity*. When you imagine the warmth of a nest and the security of being under the wings of the nurturing love of a mother hen with chicks, it paints a vivid picture of the sheltering wing of God's protection that the psalmist refers to in this passage.

Is everyone protected under the wings? Did you notice that it says,

"He will cover you with His pinions [feathers], and under His wings you *may* seek refuge"? Again, it's up to us to make that decision! We can seek refuge under His wings if we *choose* to.

The Lord gave me a vivid picture of what it means to seek refuge under His wings. My husband, Jack, and I live out in the country, and one spring our old mother hen hatched a brood of baby chickens. One afternoon when they were scattered all over the yard, I suddenly saw the shadow of a hawk overhead. Then I noticed something that taught me a lesson I will never forget. That mother hen did not run to those little chicks and jump on top of them to try to cover them with her wings. No!

Instead, she squatted down, spread out her wings and began to cluck. And those little chickens, from every direction, came running *to her* to get under those outstretched wings. Then the hen pulled her wings down tight, tucking every little chick safely under her. To get to those babies, the hawk would have to go through the mother.

When I think of those baby chicks running to their mother, I realize it is under His wings that we *may* seek refuge—but we have to run to Him. "He will cover you with His pinions, and under His wings you may seek refuge." That one little word *may* is a strong word! It is up to us! All that mother hen did was cluck and expand her wings to tell her chicks where to come. These verses show the maternal hovering side to His protection:

> Jerusalem, Jerusalem....How often I wanted to gather your children together, the way a hen gathers her chicks under her wings, and you were unwilling.
>
> —Matthew 23:37

Notice the contrast between God's willingness and our unwillingness: His *wanting* against our *not willing to*...His *would* against our *would not*. What an amazing analogy to show us that He offers protection that we don't accept!

It is interesting that Jesus uses the correlation of *maternal* love to demonstrate His attachment to us. There is a certain fierceness to motherly love we cannot overlook. God is deeply committed to us—yet at the same time, *we can reject* His outstretched arms if we so choose. It is available, but not automatic.

God does not run here and there, trying to cover us. He said, "I have made protection possible. You run to Me!" And when we do run to Him in faith, *the enemy* then has *to go through God to get to us*! What a comforting thought.

Let me give you an illustration. There was a man who hijacked a car. The woman who was driving the car had been studying Psalm 91 at church, but in the trauma of the moment, she only remembered there was something about being under the protection of His wings, so she began to holler, "Feathers, feathers." The assailant was so stunned by her reaction that he stopped in his tracks, turned on his heels, and fled for his life. But as I said, this protection is not automatic. So, how do we put this promise to work? Since we can't physically run to God, how do we do it? This psalm gives us a great analogy to the animal kingdom, but how can we put this promise into practice in our life? Just like this woman, we run to God with our mouths; we run to God with our hearts; we run to God with our faith—like those little chicks go running back to those *feathers*.

Chapter

A MIGHTY FORTRESS IS MY GOD

His faithfulness is a shield and bulwark.

—Psalm 91:4

I<small>T IS</small> G<small>OD'S</small> <small>FAITHFULNESS</small> to His promises that is our shield. It is not solely *our* faithfulness! God is faithful to the promises He has made.

When the enemy comes to whisper fearful or condemning thoughts in your mind, you can ward off his attack by saying, "My faith is strong because *I know my God is faithful*, and *His faithfulness* is my shield!"

How often I've heard people say, "I can't dwell in the shelter of God. I mess up and fall short too many times. I feel guilty and unworthy." God knows all about our weaknesses. That is why He gave His Son. We can no more earn or deserve this protection than we can earn or deserve our salvation. The main thing is that if we slip and fall, we must not stay down. Get up, repent, and get back under that shield of protection. Thankfully this verse says it is His faithfulness, not ours, that is our shield.

> If we are faithless, He remains faithful, for He cannot deny Himself.
>
> —2 TIMOTHY 2:13

My daughter once slipped and fell facedown in the busiest four-way intersection in our city. Embarrassment made her want to keep lying there so she didn't have to look up and show her face to so many people who would know her in a small town. Yet the worst thing she could have done would have been to lie there! This is a practical illustration of what it looks like when we fall. When you think of my daughter lying facedown in that busy intersection, don't ever forget that the worst thing you can do after you fall spiritually is *fail to get up*!

This verse just expresses again God's commitment and faithfulness to being our shield of protection. It is His faithfulness that gets us back on our feet and moving again. His unshakable faithfulness is a literal shield. I have an awesome mental picture of a huge shield out in front of me, completely hiding me from the enemy. The shield is God Himself. His faithfulness to His promises guarantees His shield will remain steadfast and available forever. Whether or not we stay behind that protection is our choice.

When you are doing something for God, many times you will run into interference or resistance—or sometimes a full-blown attack from the enemy. Take a boxer; who is it that climbs into the ring with him? His opponent! When we attempt to accomplish something for the kingdom, we too have an opponent who steps in the ring with us! The fact that we can feel the spiritual opposition when we are doing something to further the kingdom should not surprise us.

We had been teaching the people at church how to believe God's promises in Psalm 91 for protection. Some of the men were helping Jack to build a coffeehouse for the college students. It was a special night, because we were hosting a champion power lifter who would give his testimony that night at an outdoor crusade in front of the coffeehouse. He was known for being able to lift a car, and it was drawing the publicity. While the men were all working with Jack to finish everything for the event, there was an explosion that sounded like a bomb had detonated. Fire began flying out the top of the electric power pole, and steam came pouring out of the ground where they had dug a hole to pour cement.

Two of the men were standing in water left from rain the night before and were holding a metal stake in place while another man accidentally drove it into the main electric power line carrying seventy-two hundred volts of electricity. Can you even imagine how much electrical power that is? It knocked all the electricity off for blocks around, *yet neither man was hurt.* Just that morning, Jack had prayed a Psalm 91 shield of protection over all the workers.

Many people have been killed from the voltage of a small electrical outlet in a room. The current running through that line at the coffeehouse was many, many times more powerful than that, yet God's shield had saved the lives of those men that day. The years of quoting Psalm 91 over our church body had certainly paid off. This not only shielded the men individually but also protected the whole crusade from being a disaster.

Psalm 91:4 also tells us that God's faithfulness is our bulwark. According to *Nelson's Bible Dictionary*, a *bulwark* is "a tower built along a city wall from which defenders shoot arrows and hurl large stones at the enemy."[1] Think about that! God's faithfulness to His promises is not only a shield, but it is also a tower. From that tower God is faithful to point out the enemy so he can't sneak up on our blind side. *Webster's Dictionary* defines *bulwark* as "an earthwork or defensive wall, fortified rampart; a breakwater; the part of a ship's side above the deck."[2] If you are on board a ship, the word *bulwark* gives you a visual of His protection.

Throughout history there have been shields over individuals and groups who have stood on Psalm 91. One of the most famous examples comes from World War I about a unit that was completely protected.

On both sides of the Atlantic, religious publications reported the story of a *miracle regiment* whose soldiers went through some of the most intense and bloodiest battles without a single combat casualty. The best sources say it was a British-American combination unit rather than an American one. Our researchers have enjoyed rebuilding this bridge between this event and its sources and uncovering new leads to one of the most celebrated pulpit examples of the power of Psalm 91. Our sources say that every officer, as well as enlisted men, daily placed his trust in God by faithfully reciting Psalm 91 together, and that unit is known to have suffered not one single combat casualty. It is unthinkable to believe that mere chance or coincidence could have prevented so many bullets and shells from finding their intended victims.[3] Psalm 91 has truly been a shield for entire troops of soldiers in each of our wars since World War I. Stories keep surfacing of Psalm 91 having shielded whole units who have claimed its promises. This is the bulwark aspect of the shield of protection.

But this shield has also been a powerful promise for the individual. I'm going to share a remarkable story of how individualized this shield can be. During that dreadful yet triumphant week in May of 1940 when the British army had been forced into total retreat and lay exposed on the sandy shores of Dunkirk, many miracles occurred. Lying hopelessly exposed, pinned down by Nazi planes and heavy artillery, and armed only with their rifles, the brave troops were seemingly trapped by the channel with no place to turn for protection. A British chaplain told of lying facedown in the sand for what seemed an eternity on the shell-torn beach at Dunkirk. Nazi bombers dropped their lethal charges, causing shrapnel to kick up sand all around him, while other planes repeatedly strafed his position with their machine guns blazing.

Although dazed by the concussions around him, the British chaplain suddenly became aware that in spite of the deafening roar of the shells and bombs falling all around him, he hadn't been hit. With bullets still raining down about him, he stood and stared with amazement at the *outline of his own shape* in the sand. It was the only smooth and undisturbed spot on the entire bullet-riddled beach. His heavenly shield must have fit the exact shape of his body.[4]

Note that this verse in Psalm 91:4 declares God's faithfulness to us as both a shield and a bulwark in a double-layered analogy. The passage uses two military symbols of fortification and protection. God is our bulwark, our tower—our wall of protection in a collective sense—and He is also our shield—a very individualized defense. This verse indicates *double* protection.

Chapter

6

I WILL NOT FEAR
THE TERROR

You will not be afraid of the terror by night.
—Psalm 91:5

I T IS INTERESTING TO note that verses 5 and 6 of Psalm 91 cover an entire twenty-four-hour period, emphasizing *day-and-night* protection. But what is more important is that these two verses encompass *every evil known to man*.

The psalmist divides the list into four categories. We will look at those categories one at a time. The first, *terror by night*, includes all the evils that come through man: kidnapping, robbery, rape, murder, terrorism, and wars. It is the dread—or horror—or alarm that comes from what man can do to you. God is saying, "You will not be afraid of any of those things, because they will not approach you." The first thing verse 5 deals with is fear.

Over and over Jesus told us, "Do not fear!" Why do you think He continually reminds us not to be afraid? Because it is through faith in His Word we are protected—and since fear is the opposite of faith, the Lord knows fear will keep us from operating in the faith that is necessary to receive. It is no wonder God addresses *the fear of terror* first.

So, how do we keep from being afraid? Very simply! In Psalm 91 God gives us instructions to quiet the fear that rises in our hearts. These words, "You will not be afraid of the terror by night or of the arrow that flies by day," are also addressing the anxiety that comes the night before battle.

Fear comes when we think we are responsible for bringing about this protection ourselves. Too often we think, "Oh, if I can just believe hard enough, maybe I'll be protected!" That's wrong thinking! The protection is already there. It has already been provided, whether we receive it or not. Faith is simply the *choice to receive* what Jesus has *already* done. The Bible gives classic examples of how to deal with terror.

The answer is in the blood of Jesus. Exodus 12:23 tells us that when Israel put blood on the door facings, the destroyer could not come in. The animal blood they used serves as a *type* and *shadow*, or a picture of the blood of Jesus that ratifies our *better* protection—under our *better* covenant (Heb. 8:6).

When we confess aloud, "I am protected by the blood of Jesus"—and believe it, the devil literally cannot come in. Remember, verse 2 tells us, "I will say to the LORD, 'My refuge and my fortress.'" It is *heart and mouth*—believing with our heart and confessing with our mouth.

Our physical weapons are operated with our hands, but we operate our *spiritual* weapons with our mouths. The blood is applied by *saying it* in faith. Confessing with our mouth and believing with our heart starts with the new birth experience and sets precedence for receiving all of God's good gifts (Rom. 10:9–10).

If we find ourselves afraid of the *terror by night,* that is our barometer letting us know we are not dwelling and abiding close to the Lord in the shelter of the Most High and believing His promises. Fear comes in when we are confessing things other than what God has said. When our eyes are not on God, fear will come. But let that fear be a reminder to repent.

We walk by faith, not by sight.
—2 Corinthians 5:7

We have to choose to believe His Word more than we believe what we see—more than we believe the terror attack. Not that we deny the existence of the attack, for the attack may be very real. But God wants our faith in His Word to become more of a reality to us than what we see in the natural.

For example, the law of gravity is a fact! No one denies the existence of gravity, but just as the laws of aerodynamics can temporarily supersede the law of gravity, Satan's attacks can also be superseded by a higher law—the law of faith and obedience to God's Word. Faith does not deny the existence of *terror*. There are simply higher laws in the Bible for overcoming it.

David did not deny the existence of the giant. Fear has us compare the size of the giant to ourselves. Faith, on the other hand, had David compare the size of the giant to the size of his God. David's eyes saw *the giant*, but his faith saw *the promises*. (See 1 Samuel 17.)

Over the years as a pastor's wife, I can recall countless people who called my husband and me in an emergency situation for help. I also remember the times when God miraculously healed the broken neck of Audra's son, Skylar, after he fell from his bike…when Jennifer McCullough's missionary village was overtaken by murderers…when Mary Johnson was kidnapped and trapped in an abandoned cabin. God's promise in Psalm 91 turned every one of those potential disasters into victory. They were all close friends, and we were thrilled to have been personally involved, even though we were praying for those miracles from a distance. But none compares to those times when the terror is brought right in your front door. Of all the people brought to us, the one that stands out in our mind the most was when a wife was brought to our doorstep at gunpoint by a man, wild-eyed and out of control.

Surprised is hardly the word to describe the emotions we felt late that afternoon when we answered the frantic knock at our door to find this businessman holding his wife at gunpoint and asking to be allowed into the house. Our children, who were in their early teens, witnessed a valuable lesson that night, even though at the time I was wishing they were anywhere but there. We found out later that an all-points bulletin had been put out for this man's arrest for the abduction of his wife with a deadly weapon. Reflecting back on the situation, I had never seen two people together with such opposite expressions on their faces: his—torment; hers—terror.

It was during a fit of anger that he had brought his wife, after three and a half hours at gunpoint, to our living room. Jack, who is much calmer than I am during a crisis, simply invited them into the den and began defusing the crisis by asking questions. It is amazing how calming the effect can be when someone is given the opportunity to get his frustrations out in the open. Gradually, the young man relaxed and, in time, became comfortable enough to put his gun down, much to the relief of everyone in the room.

I love the good endings where one escapes harm, but this episode had an even more powerful outcome when Jack prayed over both of them separately, and then escorted the businessman to the police station to turn himself in. The sheriff's department later extended a warm thank-you for defusing a volatile situation because of the couple's high-profile status. I still hear from the woman from time to time, and the report is that their marriage is going well.

We do not have to be afraid of the *terror of what man can do to harm us*. Praise God for our higher law! God's laws triumph over man's laws.

Chapter

I WILL NOT FEAR THE ARROW

You will not be afraid…of the arrow that flies by day.
—Psalm 91:5

THE SECOND CATEGORY OF evil is the *arrow that flies by day.* An arrow is something that pierces or wounds spiritually, physically, mentally, or emotionally. Arrows are intentional. This category indicates you are in a *spiritual* battle zone; specific enemy assignments are directed toward your life to defeat you.

Arrows are deliberately sent by the enemy and meticulously *aimed at the spot that will cause the most damage.* They are targeted toward the area where your mind is not renewed by the Word of God. It may perhaps be an area where you are still losing your temper, where you are still easily offended, or perhaps an area of rebellion or fear!

The enemy seldom attacks us in an area where we are built up and strong. He attacks us where we're still struggling. That's why we have to run to God! And when we battle using our spiritual weapons, the enemy's arrows will not approach us.

In Ephesians 6:16, God tells us that we have a "shield of faith with which you will be able to extinguish all the flaming arrows of the evil one." This covers the area of intentional danger. Someone bends the bow and pulls back the bowstring. The arrows are aimed and released. These are not regular, everyday arrows; they are *on fire*. Yet God doesn't say we can miss most of them. He says we can extinguish *all* of them. When arrows are sent to wound us spiritually, physically, mentally, emotionally, or financially, God wants us to ask and believe by faith that He will *pick us up* and deliver us from calamity.

One of the biggest enemy assignments is something that plagues so many families, without their ever even recognizing that it originates from a demonic force. The world calls it being *accident-prone*. But there is nothing *accidental* about accidents. Even though the word *accident* paints a picture in one's mind of something quite unintentional happening randomly, it is the word itself—*accident*—that keeps us blinded to the truth.

For years Jack was plagued with one mishap after another. He worked outdoors much of the time and had such a wide variety of responsibilities that it was almost expected that he would be in a position to encounter more accidents than most men. For example, when we visited with my folks, he would take advantage of Dad's welding shop to make carton racks for Pepsi displays. Once when he was bending the heavy wire for the back of the display, it sprang out of his hand and, of all things, flew up his nose, cutting the tender inner membrane. Blood began gushing out like a fountain. We found him right before he passed out.

Another time, he was pulling a huge concession trailer back to Brownwood. Our town is located in a valley, so just as you come into the city limits you descend down one of the largest mountains around. Just as he started down the incline, the trailer came off the hitch and began to pass his truck. No one could believe that he was not killed or hurt badly in that episode. Later, as he and my father were putting a new roof on the barn, Jack went through the roof and found himself hanging by his ribs on the rafter as his feet and legs dangled below. Another time, two other guys asked him to help raise a deer blind that was made out of heavy pipe. With Jack in the middle, the three of them were all on one side of the deer blind, attempting to raise it up far enough to rock it on up to a standing position. Just as they had it up over their heads, one of the guys slipped. The two on the outside were able to run out from under the several-hundred-pound deer stand, but Jack was stuck in the middle with no place to run. That monstrosity of a deer blind came crashing down on the back of his head, bending his back in two and driving his head in the ground barely two inches from his feet. Only God could have kept his back from snapping under the pressure. Once, when he worked for the FMC Company running the heavy machinery, he couldn't get his hand out from under the drill press in time, and it drove a chuck the size of a quarter through his hand. We had been confessing for years, "The bones of the righteous shall not be broken." There was one surprised doctor when he heard what had happened and realized that the bones in Jack's hand were not broken. As the chuck came down, it had spread the carpal bones, allowing the metal to pass through without breaking a bone.

It was during that accident that God got Jack's attention and made him realize that being *accident-prone* was a demonic assignment that needed to be broken. We finally said, "It's enough." He was prayed for, and, supernaturally, the accidents stopped. I think people would be dumbfounded to realize how many times they are putting up with arrows from the enemy that they should never have had to endure.

There are many types of enemy arrows. My daughter, Angie, and her husband, David, were living in Irving while he attended chiropractor school. One particular Sunday after church, several couples were putting their lunch together. Everyone was making jokes about Julee missing church and being late for the lunch: "Where is she? She is supposed to be bringing the dessert." Who could have known that she was having the fight of her life and *winning* one of the strongest victories over rape that I have ever heard. And to think that we were all just thinking about our stomachs. What a witness that God's Word is more powerful than assault. It is able to extinguish every flaming arrow. (See her testimony on page 138.)

We have a *covenant* with God telling us *not to be afraid of the arrow that flies by day*. Assignments will rise up, but don't be afraid of the arrows. God has promised they will not hit their target.

Chapter

I WILL NOT BE AFRAID OF THE PESTILENCE

You will not be afraid...of the pestilence that stalks in darkness.

—Psalm 91:5–6

F EAR GRIPPED MY HEART, and beads of perspiration popped out on my forehead as I feverishly ran my fingers over what felt like a lump in my body. How I dreaded the monthly self-examination that the doctor had suggested. My fingertips were as cold as ice from the panic I had worked up just thinking about what I might find and dreading the turn my life might take from there.

On that particular day it turned out to be a false alarm, but the dread of what I might find in the coming months was constantly in the back of my mind until this promise came alive in my heart. If you fight fears of fatal diseases, then this is the scripture for you to take hold of.

The third category of evil God names is *pestilence*. This is the only evil He names twice! Since God doesn't waste words, He must have a specific reason for repeating this promise.

Have you noticed that when a person says something more than once, it is usually because that person wants to emphasize a point? God knew the pestilence and the fear that would be running rampant in these end days. The world is teeming with fatal epidemics hitting people by the thousands, so God catches our attention by repeating this promise.

It's as though God is saying, "I said in verse 3, 'You are delivered from the deadly pestilence,' but did you really hear Me? Just to be sure, I am saying it again in verse 6, '*You do not have to be afraid of the deadly pestilence*'!" This is so contrary to what the world teaches us that we have to renew our thinking. Only then can we comprehend the fact that we do not have to be afraid of the sicknesses and the disease epidemics in the world today.

When I first started studying this psalm, I remember thinking, "I don't know whether I have the faith to believe these promises!" This thought stretched my faith and my mind until I thought it would snap like a rubber band that was being pulled too tightly.

God, however, reminded me that *faith is not a feeling*. Faith is simply *choosing* to believe what He says in His Word. The more I chose to believe God's Word, the more I had a *knowing* I could trust and rely on it completely.

Our inheritance is not limited to what is handed down to us genetically from our ancestors. Our inheritance can be what Jesus provided for us if we believe the Word and put it to work.

> Christ redeemed us from the curse of the Law, having become a curse for us.
>
> —GALATIANS 3:13

The pestilence mentioned in Psalm 91:6 is spelled out in detail in Deuteronomy 28. This scripture in Galatians tells us we are *redeemed* from every curse (including pestilence) if we will believe and appropriate the promise.

Never before in our history has there been so much talk of *terrorism* and *germ warfare*, but to the surprise of so many people, God is not shocked or caught off guard by these things. Do we think chemical warfare is bigger than God? Long before man ever discovered biological weapons, God made provision for the protection of His people—if they would believe His Word.

> These signs will accompany those who have believed...if they drink any deadly poison, it will not hurt them.
> —Mark 16:17–18

According to *Strong's Concordance*, the word *drink* in this scripture comes from the Greek word *pino*, meaning "imbibe."[1] *Imbibe* means "to drink, to absorb, to inhale or to take into the mind."[2] No evil has been conceived by man against which God has not provided a promise of protection for any of His children who will choose to believe it and act on it.

What about the fear that has come on mankind regarding our polluted water supplies or foods contaminated by pesticides? I believe the Word of God advocates using wisdom, but all the precautions in the world cannot protect us from every harmful thing that could be in our food and water. I am sure you have all found yourselves in conditions where the food and water were questionable. Therefore, God's instruction to bless our food and water before eating is not simply some ritual to make us look more spiritual; rather, it is another provision for our safety, playing an important role in God's protective plan.

> But the Spirit explicitly says that in later times...men...[will] advocate abstaining from foods which God has created to be gratefully shared in by those who believe and know the truth. For everything created by God is good, and nothing is to be rejected if it is received with gratitude; *for it is sanctified by means of the word of God and prayer.*
> —1 Timothy 4:1, 3–5, emphasis added

But you shall serve the Lord your God, and He will *bless your bread and your water*; and I will *remove sickness from your midst.*
—Exodus 23:25, emphasis added

It is God's goodness that made these provisions before we ever asked! This is not for everyone; it is for those *who believe and know the truth.* Blessing the food with gratitude literally brings about sanctification—or a cleansing of our food and water.

In biblical days when they mentioned pestilence, they were thinking of diseases such as leprosy. Luke 21:11 states that one of the signs of the End Times is an outbreak of pestilence. And today we have many widespread diseases such as AIDS, cancer, malaria, heart disease, and tuberculosis; but no matter what pestilence we might be facing, His promise never ceases to be true.

The enemy may try to cause sudden surprises to catch us unaware and knock us down, but God is faithful. His Word is true no matter what the circumstances look like at times. For example, I have never seen anyone stand as steadfastly as my close friend Rene Hood when the doctor diagnosed her with the last stages of lupus. Some of her major organs were shutting down, and the doctors had given up. As a pastor's wife, I cannot tell you how much I was dreading the phone calls, when every day she seemed to be getting so close to death's door. But she refused to turn loose of God's covenant promise of deliverance from pestilence. More than ten years later, she is still alive and well, against all odds, and preaching the Word of God in churches and prisons all over the nation. Some people receive an instantaneous gift of healing, but Rene took it by persistence—by refusing to let go of her promises of healing and inch by inch claiming God's covenant protection. Some think they need a special word to claim a certain promise in the Bible, but Rene counted God's Word as written just for her.

What a joy it was two years ago when she and I went together to the Philippines to tag-team teach at seminars. We went by pump boat to one of the remote islands and arrived several hours after the seminar was supposed to start. No one seemed to mind. The precious ladies were patiently waiting there for us. In fact, one of the ladies had waded several miles through low tide just to get to the meeting. Our clothes were dirty from the long trip by pump boat, and we had perspired badly in the tropical heat, but no one seemed to notice when we began to bring the Word of God. Rene's doctor keeps careful watch over her. In fact, he had told her not to go to some remote place overseas, but she was not about to let a worried doctor keep her from doing what God had called her to do. When she came home, the tests that he ran showed that her immune system was completely normal. Don't let a fear of pestilence keep you from the will of God. (See Rene's testimony on page 177.)

Fear of illness was probably my biggest battle in my mind. Out of all that Psalm 91 has done for me, it was this passage that caused me to overcome. I shudder to think what we might open ourselves up to without the promise of Psalm 91 and without the determination to stand firm and refuse to entertain fearful thoughts. What we allow our mind to dwell on is *our* choice. Therefore if we desire to operate in this protection covenant, taking authority over negative thoughts and emotions is imperative. It is amazing how the simple phrase "I am just not going there" will dispel those fear thoughts immediately.

I am sure this promise of protection from plagues and pestilence reminded the Jews of Israel's complete immunity from the Egyptian plagues in the land of Goshen. The destroyer could not come in where the blood was applied. Even in the Old Testament God declared: "You will not be afraid…of the pestilence that stalks in darkness… *it shall not approach you*" (Ps. 91:5–7, emphasis added).

Chapter

9

I WILL NOT FEAR THE DESTRUCTION

You will not be afraid... of the destruction that lays waste at noon.

—PSALM 91:5–6

THIS FOURTH CATEGORY OF evil is *destruction*. Destruction encompasses the *evils over which mankind has no control*, those things the world ignorantly calls *acts of God*—tornadoes, floods, hail, hurricanes, or fire! God very plainly tells us we are not to fear destruction. These natural disasters are not from God.

In Mark 4:39, Jesus rebuked the storm, and it became perfectly calm. This demonstrates that God is not the author of such things; otherwise, Jesus would never have contradicted His Father by rebuking something sent by Him.

There is no place in the world you can go and be safe from every *destruction*—every natural disaster. We can never anticipate what might come when we least expect it. But no matter where you are in the world, God says to run to His shelter where you will not be afraid of the *destruction—it will not approach you!*

Our granddaughter Jolena and her husband, Heath Adams, were stationed in Turkey just before the war was declared in Iraq. Soon after her arrival in Turkey, Jolena started working as a lifeguard at a pool. One day at the end of June, she began to hear a loud noise that sounded much like a plane breaking the sound barrier; then everything started to shake. Everyone around her began to panic when the water splashed in the pool from an earthquake, which was later found to be 6.3 on the Richter scale. Swimmers tried desperately to get out of the water to find some place of safety, while children clung to Jolena and screamed in fear. Everywhere people were hollering, but Jolena said she felt a peace and a calm come over her. She started praying in a loud voice, pleading the blood of Jesus over the air force base and over the people there. Suddenly, everyone around her became perfectly quiet and listened to her prayer. No one on the base was seriously hurt, but just five minutes away apartment buildings had collapsed. More than a thousand people were killed in the quake. Heath was at work as he watched the wall of a building completely crumble and fall to the street.

Every day Jolena and Heath had been praying Psalm 91 protection over their home, and it certainly paid off. The base suffered a great deal of structural damage; the PX (post exchange) and the gym were completely lost, and many of the houses were destroyed. Not only were houses destroyed, but also furniture, TVs, and stereos were ruined as well, causing literally thousands of dollars in damage. Because of large cracks caused by the earthquake, you could actually see through the walls of many of the houses. On a home just one block from Jolena and Heath, the staircase had completely separated from the wall. Their miracle was that other than one tiny crack over one of the doorways, there was not one bit of damage to their house or to any of their furnishings. While many of their friends had to move out of their homes while they were repaired, Jolena and Heath didn't have to go through any of that.

God wants us to take seriously His promise that *we do not have to fear destruction; it will not approach us.*

The dangers from destruction can approach quickly and in broad daylight; therefore, you must know your covenant promises. One day, Jack and our son, Bill, were burning brush—not knowing there was an old underground gas well at the back of our three-hundred-acre property. As you can imagine, when the fire reached over the gas well, it literally exploded, sending fire in every direction and igniting a nearby grass field. Immediately the fire was completely out of control. With no water lines back there at the time, Jack and Bill were fighting to no avail. The barrel of water they had in the back of the pickup didn't even make a dent in the flames.

Seeing the fire was getting dangerously close to other fields that fed right into the surrounding homes, Jack hurried up to the house to call the fire department, sending me to meet the firemen at the crossroads so they wouldn't get lost, and dashed back, only to find that the fire was out. Bill, looking as though he had been working in the coal mines, was sitting on a tree stump trying to catch his breath. Jack said, "How on earth were you able to put out the fire? There was no way!"

Bill's next words—"I called on God"—said it all. You too can be delivered from *destruction at noon.* For those out-of-control days, God is always there.

Did you know that every evil known to man will fall into one of these four categories we have named in chapters 6 through 9 (verses 5–6 of Psalm 91): terror, arrows, pestilence, or destruction? And the amazing thing is that God has offered us deliverance from them all.

God has said in His Word that we will not be afraid of *terror, arrows, pestilence, or destruction*...these things *will not approach us*—if we *dwell in His shelter and abide in His shadow.* This psalm is not filled with exceptions or vague conditions as if trying to give God an out or an excuse to fail to fulfill the promises. Rather, it is a bold statement of what He *wants* to do for us.

We can receive anything God has already provided. The secret is in knowing that everything for which God has made provision is clearly spelled out and defined in the Word of God. *If you can find where God has offered it, you can have it!* It is never God holding it back. His provision is already there—waiting to be received.

God is faithful to all the promises He has made. He didn't create man and then leave man to himself. When He created us, He automatically made Himself responsible to care for us and meet our every need. And when He makes a promise, He is faithful to what He has promised. This psalm seems to build from one promise to the next. Men are judged by their faithfulness to their own word. Real men are only as good as their word. God is more faithful than even the most truthful man, for He has the power to carry out His Word.

Faith is not a tool to manipulate God into giving you something *you* want. Faith is simply the means by which we accept what God has already made available. Our goal needs to be the *renewal* of our minds to such an extent that we have more faith in God's Word than in what we perceive with our physical senses. God does not make promises that are out of our reach.

When the Lord first began showing me these promises, and my mind was still struggling with "How can this be?"—*doubts*—He took me to a portion of His Word that helped to set me free:

> What then? If some did not believe, their unbelief will not nullify the faithfulness of God, will it? May it never be! Rather, let God be found true, though every man be found a liar, as it is written, "That you may...prevail when you are judged."
> —ROMANS 3:3–4

God is telling us that even though there may be some who *don't believe*, their unbelief will never nullify His promises to the ones who *do believe*. Paul in Romans, quoting from the Old Testament, gives us an important reminder that what we as individuals choose to believe and confess will cause us to prevail during a time of judgment.

Without the promises of protection throughout the Word of God, and especially without our Psalm 91 covenant—*listing all forms of protection made available in one psalm*—we might feel rather presumptuous if, on our own, we asked God to protect us from all the things listed in these last four verses. (Review chapters 6–9 of this book.) In fact, we probably would not have the nerve to ask for all of this coverage. But He offered this protection to us before we even had a chance to ask!

THOUGH A THOUSAND FALL

A thousand may fall at your side
And ten thousand at your right hand,
But it shall not approach you....
For you have made the LORD, my refuge,
Even the Most High, your dwelling place.

—PSALM 91:7, 9

D
O WE EVEN STOP to consider what God is saying to us in verse 7? Do we have the courage to trust God's Word enough to believe *He means this literally*? Is it possible for this to be true and for us to miss out on these promises?

Jesus answers the last question in Luke 4:27: "There were many lepers in Israel in the time of Elisha the prophet; and none of them was cleansed." Only Naaman, the Syrian, was healed when he obeyed in faith. *Not everyone will receive the benefits of this promise in Psalm 91.*

Only those who believe God and hold fast to His promises will profit; nonetheless, it *is* available. To the measure we trust Him, we will in the same measure reap the benefits of that trust.

What an awesome statement! God wants us to know that even though there will be a thousand falling by our side and ten thousand at our right hand, it does not negate the promise that destruction will not approach the one who chooses to believe and trust His Word. God means exactly what He says.

Have you ever been fishing on a lake in the middle of the night? Some people think that is the very best time to catch fish. When my husband was seven years old, all the people who worked for his father took their boats to Lake Brownwood to do some night fishing. Jack was placed in a boat with five adults so he would be well supervised. Since one of the men in the boat was an expert swimmer, his mother and dad thought he would be in especially good hands.

Later that night, during one of the times when the boats were going back and forth to shore for bait, Jack had gotten out of his boat and into another one without anyone noticing. Then off they went—without Jack—back onto the lake in the dark. This was back before there were rules about life jackets and lights on your fishing boats, so no one could see in the dark what actually happened. Perhaps they hit a stump. But for some reason the boat Jack had been in sank. All five of the people in it drowned, even the expert swimmer. It became obvious that Jack had been directed to another boat by an unseen hand.

Disaster can strike suddenly when everything is going well, and it can really break your heart to see times when thousands fall. This is why the promises in Psalm 91 are so important to you.

It is no accident that the little statement "it shall not approach you" is tucked right here in the middle of the psalm. Have you noticed how easy it is to become fearful when disaster strikes all around you? We begin to feel like Peter must have felt as he walked on the water to Jesus. It is easy to see how he started sinking into the waves when he saw all the turbulence of the storm going on around him.

God knew there would be times when we would hear so many

negative reports, see so many needs, and encounter so much danger around us we would feel overwhelmed. That is why He warned us ahead of time that thousands would be falling all around us. He did not want us to be caught off guard. But at that point we have a choice to make. The ball is then in our court! We can either choose to run to His shelter in faith, and the storm will not approach us, or we can passively live our lives the way the world does, not realizing there is something we can do about it.

Psalm 91 is the *preventive* measure that God has given to His children against every evil known to mankind. No place else in the Word are all of the protection promises (including help from angels, as well as promises insuring our authority) accumulated in one covenant to offer such a total package for living in this world. It is both an *offensive* and *defensive measure* for warding off every evil before it has had time to strike. This is not only a *cure* but also a plan for *complete prevention*!

What tremendous insight after our minds have been renewed by the Word of God to realize, contrary to the world's thinking, we do not have to be among the ten thousand who fall at our right hand.

You will only look on with your eyes
And see the recompense of the wicked.

—Psalm 91:8

You will see recompense (payment) being doled out at times. There is judgment. Sooner or later every sin will be exposed and paid for. An evil dictator falls, an unrighteous aggressor is stopped, a tyrant faces his crimes against humanity, a wrong is rectified—the *recompense of the wicked speaks of justice.* Wars have been fought where one side had a righteous cause and, consequently, good won over evil. The justice of God is that evil will not triumph—that Hitlers do not win, that communistic governments fall, that darkness does not extinguish light.

Verse 8 says that we will "only look on and see" it happening. The word *only* denotes a protection of only seeing and not experiencing the evil, and it denotes detachment in that the evil we *see* does not get inside of us. We are set apart in that we do not allow our enemy's hate to change us.

Let's look for just a moment at this scripture with our faith in mind; do we sometimes fall short into unbelief? Faith in God, in His Son Jesus Christ, and in His Word is *counted* in God's eyes as righteousness. But when we are in unbelief, to a degree we are placing ourselves in the category of the *wicked*. Sometimes, even as a Christian, I have been an *unbelieving* believer when it comes to receiving *all* of God's Word.

Jesus says in Matthew 5:18: "Not the smallest letter or stroke shall pass from the Law until all is accomplished." Even if believers have never utilized this psalm in its full potential, the truth has never passed away or lost one ounce of its power.

Many people think of the gospel as an insurance policy, securing only their eternity and their comfort after disaster strikes. They are depriving themselves of so much. Perhaps we all need to ask ourselves the question: "What kind of coverage do I have—fire or life?" God's Word is more than merely an escape from hell; it is a handbook for living a victorious life *in this world*.

Jesus lived in a realm where He literally was not approached by evil. There is a difference between the destruction of the enemy and persecution for the gospel's sake. Paul writes in 2 Timothy 3:12: "All who desire to live godly in Christ Jesus will be persecuted." There are times when we will be mistreated because of our stand for the cause of Christ. Psalm 91 is a very distinct concept dealing with natural disasters, accidents, sickness, and destruction. Jesus suffered persecution, but He did not face calamity, disaster, and mishap. Accidents never even *approached* Him. This distinction is easy to understand if you separate persecution from freak accidents and mishaps.

There is a place where calamity literally does not even approach us. This would be seemingly impossible to imagine—especially in combat situations. Yet to look at this verse in its true context, *with thousands falling on either side*, we observe the strongest description of casualty and calamity named in the psalm. If this verse isn't a description of actual combat, I don't know what is. Yet tied to it is a promise of protection beyond anything that could otherwise be envisioned. This portrayal of *people falling* is directly connected to the promise that *it will not even come near us*. Two opposite poles joined together!

Too many people see Psalm 91 as a beautiful promise that they file right alongside all of their other quality reading material. It makes them feel comforted every time they read it. But I do not want anyone to read this book and fail to see the *superior significance* to these promises in this psalm. These are not written for our inspiration but for our protection. These are not words of comfort *in* affliction but words of deliverance *from* affliction.

Chapter

NO PLAGUE COMES NEAR MY FAMILY

There shall no evil befall you, nor any plague or calamity come near your tent.

—Psalm 91:10, amp

ARE YOU WORRIED ABOUT the welfare of your family? This part of Psalm 91 is written just for you. After God repeats our part of the condition in verse 9, He then reemphasizes the promise in verse 10: "Nor shall any plague come near your dwelling" (nkjv). It is at this point in the psalm that the Bible makes this covenant more comprehensive than merely being about ourselves!

God has just added a *new dimension* to the promise—the opportunity to exercise faith not only for ourselves but also for the protection of our entire household. If these promises were only available to us as individuals, they would not be completely comforting. Because God has created within us both an instinct to be protected and a need to protect those who belong to us, He has assured us here that these promises are for each of us and our *households*.

It appears that the Old Testament leaders had a better understanding of this concept than we who are under the new covenant. That is why Joshua chose for himself *and for his household*.

> If it is disagreeable in your sight to serve the LORD, choose for yourselves today whom you will serve...but as for me *and my house*, we will serve the LORD.
>
> —JOSHUA 24:15, EMPHASIS ADDED

As Joshua made the decision that his household would serve God with him, he was influencing their destiny and declaring their protection at the same time. In much the same way, Rahab bargained with the Israeli spies for her whole family (Josh. 2:13).

When our hearts are truly steadfast, and we are trusting in His faithfulness to fulfill His promises, we will not be constantly afraid something bad will happen to one of our family members.

> He will not fear evil tidings;
> His heart is steadfast, trusting in the LORD.
>
> —PSALM 112:7

Negative expectations will begin to pass away, and we will start expecting good reports. According to this verse, we can grab our ears and proclaim, "These ears were made to hear good tidings!" The fear of bad tidings can plague our very existence, things like the fear of the phone ringing in the night, of that knock on the door, of the siren of an ambulance, or of that letter of condolence. This verse promises that a steadfast heart will not live in constant fear of tragic news. Someone once said, "Fear knocked at the door, and faith answered. No one was there."[1] When fear knocks, let your mouth say aloud, "I will not fear evil tidings; my heart is steady, trusting in You!"

We exercise a certain amount of authority for those *under our roof.* Our family has had several notable experiences of God delivering people from calamity who were on our land, in our home, or *near our dwelling*. In one illustration of this, our grandson, Heath Adams, had gone hunting with one of his buddies. Upon seeing a coyote, the friend traded places with Heath and jumped in the passenger seat of the pickup for a better view. Since the bipod on his rifle was longer than the gun barrel, he couldn't put the barrel down, so he rested the .30-06 rifle between his legs, facing up. Somehow the jostling of the pickup caused the gun to fire, sending a 180-grain bullet through his chest and armpit. The friend started screaming he had been hit, and to Heath's dismay, all he saw was a bloody mass of muscle and tissue. The concussion from the blast alone was so strong it blew out the back window. In an instant, Heath pulled off his jacket, put it under his friend's arm, and then applied pressure to the arm and chest wound in an effort to stop the bleeding. Simultaneously, holding pressure against the arm and gripping the steering wheel to hold it steady, he drove rapidly on the icy road, all the while searching for service with his cell phone—all without mishap. It was nothing short of a miracle.

Heath was able to get through with his cell phone to the 911 dispatcher, but he still had to drive the twenty-two-mile stretch to the nearest town. That too may have been part of God's plan, because it gave him time to declare God's promise from Psalm 91. Heath said later that he was not about to let his friend die. His friend was not *born again*, and he was determined that no flaming arrow of the enemy was going to take his buddy out before he made Jesus the Lord of his life. The whole ordeal was miraculous, as the friend underwent six hours of surgery and came out with no permanent damage.

God was certainly at work that day. Normally it would have been disastrous to drive fifty or sixty miles per hour on an icy, Montana road in December—especially while steering left-handed during a life-and-death situation. But Heath said no matter how fast he drove, God gave the pickup enough traction so that never once was there even a hint of the wheels sliding. Later they went back to the same place, and try as they might, they could not get cell phone service anywhere in that twenty-two-mile trek. Of course, the biggest miracle of all was that a bullet wound through the chest and arm neither hit a vital organ nor damaged his arm beyond repair. Heath's friend was blessed beyond words to have been with someone who knew and loved God and held fast to God's Word.

In Matthew 13:32, Jesus makes reference to the mustard seed starting as an herb but growing into a tree with the birds nesting in the branches. Others can find protection in our faith as well when we plant the seed of the Word.

The beauty of this psalm is that when someone prays for more than himself, he brings the entire family under the shield of God's Word. It introduces an added dimension to us as individuals to be able to apply the richness of this covenant to our entire household.

Late one night, soon after building our new home in the country, our family was faced with a severe weather alert. The local radio station warned that a tornado had been sighted just south of the country club—the exact location of our property. We could see several of the React Club vehicles parked on the road below our hill as the members watched the funnel cloud that seemed to be headed straight for our house.

I had never seen such a strange, eerie color in the night sky or experienced such a deafening silence in the atmosphere. You could actually feel the hair on your body stand on end. Some of our son's friends were visiting, and to their surprise, Jack quickly ordered our family to get outside with our Bibles (even though we were in our pajamas) and start circling the house—quoting Psalm 91 and taking authority over the storm. Jack had our children out speaking directly to the storm, just as Jesus did.

The eerie silence suddenly turned into a roar, with torrents of rain coming down in what seemed like bucketfuls. Finally Jack had a peace the danger had passed, even though by sight nothing had changed.

We walked back into the house just in time to hear the on-location reporter call the radio announcer and exclaim over the air, with so much excitement he was almost shouting, "This is nothing short of a miracle—the funnel cloud south of the Brownwood Country Club has suddenly lifted up and vanished into the clouds."

You should have seen those kids jumping and hollering. It was the first time my son's friends had observed the supernatural at work. However, their surprise was no greater than that of my daughter's college professor the next day. He asked the students in his class what they were doing during the storm. Several said they were in the bathtub under a mattress. Some were in closets, and one was in a storm cellar!

You can imagine the astonishment when he got around to our daughter, Angelia, who said, "With the tornado headed in our direction, my family was circling the house, quoting from Psalm 91: 'We will not be afraid...of the destruction that lays waste....A thousand will fall at your side, ten thousand at your right hand, but it will *not approach us....No evil will befall you, nor will any plague or calamity come near your dwelling.*'"

What a joy to know you have promises in Psalm 91 that will protect not only you but also those in your family and *near your dwelling*, as well.

ANGELS ARE
WATCHING OVER ME

For He will give His angels charge concerning you,
To guard you in all your ways.
They will bear you up in their hands,
That you do not strike your foot against a stone.
—PSALM 91:11–12

IN VERSES 11 AND 12, God makes another unique promise concerning an additional dimension of our protection. This is one of the most precious promises of God, and He put it right here in Psalm 91. In fact, this is one of the promises Satan used to test Jesus.

Most Christians read past this promise with very little, if any, thought about the magnitude of what is being said. Only after we get to heaven will we realize all the things from which we were spared because of the intervention of God's angels on our behalf.

I am sure you have read stories about missionaries whose lives were spared because would-be murderers saw large bodyguards protecting them when, in fact, there was no one there in the natural. The same is true with soldiers who have had similar experiences in combat. We have to wonder what the Iraqi soldier saw as he was poised and ready to launch his RPG into Zebulon Batke's Humvee in Baghdad. He suddenly stopped in mid-action, stared at something, then shouted at his comrade, causing them both to turn and run for their lives.[1]

We can all recall close calls where we escaped a tragedy and there was no explanation in the natural. It is possible "[to entertain] angels without knowing it," as it says in Hebrews 13:2. Sadly, I believe most Christians have a tendency to disregard the ministry of angels altogether.

Several famous writers, including C. S. Lewis,[2] have alluded to the battle at Mons, Belgium, where a great number of the British soldiers reported having seen what they all called *an intervention by angels* who came to their aid against the Germans in August 1914. According to the reports of these soldiers, this angelic assistance could not have come at a more perfect moment as they were being overrun by persistent German advancement. There is a similar version of the Mons story told by German prisoners who described what they called an army of ghosts armed with bows and arrows and led by a very tall figure on a white horse who urged the English troops to go forward. Many diaries and letters show that by 1915, the British had accepted the belief that a supernatural event had, indeed, taken place. Military historians who have studied this Belgium battle scene have enthusiastically incorporated the appearance of the angels at Mons into their writings. In another account of the battle in Mons, some Coldstream Guards, who were the last to withdraw, had become lost in the area of the Mormal Forest and had dug in to make a last stand. An angel appeared and led them across an open field to a hidden, sunken road, which enabled them to escape. Truly, England has had a long history of linking the heavenly to the military.[3]

A modern-day example involves someone we know personally. Floyd Bowers, a close friend of ours who worked in the mines of Clovis, New Mexico, had the responsibility of setting off the explosives. One particular day he was ready to push the switch when someone tapped him on the shoulder. To his surprise no one was anywhere around. Deciding it must have been his imagination, he prepared once again to detonate the dynamite, but he felt another tap on his shoulder. Again, no one was there. Floyd decided to move all the ignition equipment several hundred feet back up the tunnel. When he finally plunged the charger, the whole top of the tunnel caved in exactly where he had been standing. A coincidence? You could never make our friend believe that. He knew *someone* had tapped him on the shoulder.

Are you in harm's way? Do you feel alone? You are not alone; God has given His angels—personal heavenly bodyguards to protect you. More are fighting for you than against you.

Verse 11 of Psalm 91 says: "For He will give His angels *charge* concerning you" (emphasis added). What does that mean? Think with me for a moment. Have you ever taken charge of a situation? When you take charge of something, you put yourself in a place of leadership. You begin telling everyone what to do and how to do it. If angels are taking charge of the things that concern us, God has given the angels the authority to act on our behalf. That same truth is repeated in Hebrews.

> Are they [angels] not all ministering spirits, sent out to render service for the sake of those who will inherit salvation?
>
> —HEBREWS 1:14

When we look to God as the source of our protection and provision, the angels are constantly *rendering us aid* and *taking charge* of our affairs. Psalm 103:20 says: "…His angels, mighty in strength…obeying the voice of His Word!" As we proclaim God's Word, the angels hasten to carry it out.

Verse 11 of Psalm 91 also says that angels will "*guard* you in all your ways." Have you ever seen a soldier standing guard, protecting someone? That soldier stands at attention—alert, watchful, and ready to protect at the first sign of attack. How much more will God's angels stand *guard* over God's children, alert and ready to protect them at all times? Do we believe that? Have we even thought about it? Faith is what releases this promise to work on our behalf. How comforting it is to know God has placed these heavenly guards to have charge over us.

Psalm 91 names so many different avenues through which God protects us. It is exciting to realize from this Old Testament psalm that protection is not just a random idea in God's mind—He is committed to it. Angelic protection is another one of the *unique* ways in which God has provided that protection. What an unusual idea to add actual beings designed to protect us. He has charged angels *to guard us in all our ways*.

Chapter

13

THE ENEMY IS UNDER MY FEET

You will tread upon the lion and cobra,
The young lion and the serpent ["dragon," KJV] you
will trample down.

—PSALM 91:13

HERE IN VERSE 13 God transitions to another topic. He takes us from the subject of our protection *by Him* and puts emphasis on *the authority in His name* that has been given to us as believers.

Make a note of the corresponding New Testament scripture dealing with the authority that He has given to us:

Behold, I [Jesus] have given you authority to tread on serpents and scorpions, and over all the power of the enemy, and nothing will injure you.

—LUKE 10:19

We, as Christians, have been given authority over the enemy. *He does not have authority over us!* We need to take the time to allow that awesome reality to soak in. However, our authority over the enemy is not automatic.

My husband believes that too few Christians ever use their authority. Too often they *pray* when they should be *taking authority!* For the most part, Jesus prayed at night and took authority all day. It is not the time to start praying when we encounter the enemy; we need to be already *prayed up* by then. When we encounter the enemy, it is the time we need to speak forth the authority we have in the name of Jesus.

If a gunman suddenly faced you, would you be confident enough in your authority that you could boldly declare, "I am in covenant with the living God, and I have a blood covering that protects me from anything you might attempt to do. So, in the name of Jesus, I command you to put down that gun"?

If we do not have that kind of courage, then we need to meditate on the authority scriptures until we become confident in who we are *in Christ.* At new birth we immediately have enough power placed at our disposal to tread upon the enemy without being harmed. Most Christians, however, either do not know it, or they fail to use it. How often do we believe the Word enough to act on it?

Let's look at what this verse is actually saying. What good does it do to have authority over lions and cobras unless we are in Africa or India or someplace like that? What *does* it mean when it says that we will tread on the lion, the young lion, the cobra, and the serpent (translated as *dragon* in the King James Version of the Bible)? These words are graphic representations of things that are potentially harmful in our daily lives. They amount to unforgettable ways of describing the different types of satanic oppression that come against us. So, what do these terms mean to us today? Let's break them down.

1. Lion problems

First of all, we can encounter *lion problems*—these problems are bold, loud, and forthright, and they come out in the open to hit us head-on. At one time or another we have all had something blatant and overt come against us. It might have been a car wreck or a face-to-face encounter with the enemy on the battlefield. It might have been an unexpected bill at the end of the month, causing a chain reaction of bounced checks. Those are *lion* problems—obvious difficulties that often seem insurmountable. Yet God says we will tread on them; they will not tread on us.

2. Young lion problems

The *young lions* are less obvious, smaller issues that can grow into full-scale problems if we don't handle them. These young lion problems come to harass and destroy us gradually like little foxes! Subtle negative thoughts that tell us we will not survive or that our mate no longer loves us or that we are no longer in love with our mate are good examples of this category. Those little foxes will grow into big ones if they are not taken captive and destroyed (2 Cor. 10:4–5). Answer those little foxes with the Word of God. Small harassments, distractions, and irritations are young lions.

> Catch the foxes for us,
> The little foxes that are ruining the vineyards,
> While our vineyards are in blossom.
> —Song of Solomon 2:15

3. Cobra problems

God names *cobra* problems next. These are the problems that seem to sneak up on us like a *snake in the grass* throughout our day. They are what we might call an *undercover* attack that brings sudden death—a deceptive scheme keeping us blinded until it devours us. A surprise military ambush, failure to distinguish the enemy from a civilian, a Dear John letter—these are examples of *cobra* problems. Thank the Lord we have authority to tread over such things so these surprise attacks will not overpower us.

How many times have you witnessed a marriage unexpectedly fall apart so suddenly you couldn't imagine what had happened—only to find out later there had been underlying problems going on behind the scenes? By the time the cause was uncovered, the poison had had its effect on its victims. There is a lot of pressure on marriage in today's world, and Satan's cobra attacks are behind most of those vulnerabilities—pornography, failure to keep the marriage bed holy, adultery, homosexuality, and even long working hours that create distance in the family. At first, those things are hard to detect and are similar to the puncture wounds from cobra fangs. Although no one sees the poison as it travels through a body, the results are always damaging and, oftentimes, deadly. Only God's restoration and forgiveness can undo those attacks once they have occurred.

Sometimes in life things can happen so fast that we don't have time to pray before it is too late. What can you do when the attack is swift and deadly and takes you by surprise? Our granddaughter Jolena's story of a near tragic accident involving her daughter, Peyton, is an example of a cobra attack. One of the close friends of our family had lost a child in a very tragic accident, so it has always been on our minds and hearts. After this event, Jolena told us that she had always prayed Psalm 91, but she had recently begun to pray preventatively over her children regarding bicycles and car accidents. She didn't merely *instruct* her children in safety rules, but at least once a week she claimed that nothing like this would ever have the ability to strike. Well, the *cobra* tried, but preventative prayer over this specific sneaky type of attack paid off! (See Jolena's testimony on page 132.)

We definitely need God's protection from *cobra* attacks.

4. Dragon problems

We might have guessed the previous figurative examples, but what are the *dragon* problems? I looked up the Hebrew word in *Strong's Concordance*, and it listed *sea monster*.[1] First of all, there is no such thing as a dragon or a sea monster. Dragons are a figment of one's imagination. But have you ever experienced fears that were a figment of your imagination? Sure you have. We all have!

Dragon problems represent our unfounded fears—phantom or mirage fears. That sounds harmless enough, but are you aware that phantom fears can be as deadly as reality fears if we believe them?

Some people's *dragon* fears are as real to them as another person's *lion* problems. That is why it is important to define your fears. So many people spend all of their lives running from something that is not even chasing them. Many people allow a *lion* problem they have already faced to become a *phantom* problem they battle the rest of their lives.

> The wicked flee when no one is pursuing.
>
> —Proverbs 28:1

This verse is a good definition of phantom fears. We have had a great many people share testimonies of God's deliverance from things like fear of the unknown, fear of facing the future alone, fear of loss, fear of death, tormenting suspicions, claustrophobia, and so forth.

This category of dragon fears takes in all the vain imaginations. When Angelia was on a mission trip that involved smuggling Bibles into a communist country, the Bibles for the underground church were made available to the group to take across the border. Angelia was shocked at how many in the group, at the last minute, said they heard *God* tell them not to take any Bibles across instead of just admitting they were afraid. Later, however, when they found that 100 percent of the Bibles that were taken had made it successfully across the border through divine intervention, they had to face the fact that vain imaginations had caused them to miss out on being a part of the success of getting Bibles to the underground church. How many people have thought, "God told me," when, in fact, it was no more than a vain imagination covering a fear. I have known so many people who said they couldn't volunteer at a state correctional school because they thought they might get caught in a riot, or they couldn't go on a mission trip because they might contact some kind of disease, and even those who felt they couldn't evangelize because they might be asked a question they couldn't answer. What opportunities for the Lord have we missed because of vain imagination *dragon* fears?

Dragon fear is a very valid form of spiritual attack—especially for soldiers who have been subjected to extended periods of intense battle. When my daughter and her husband were first married, they lived in an apartment that was managed by a Vietnam veteran. Angelia came up behind him one day to bring their rent check, and he went into *attack mode*. Afterward he apologized profusely, but his body was still living in a past time zone. He was out of danger, but he was still dwelling there. Others experience mental gymnastics and restless nights—rehearsing all the things that can go wrong in each situation. Dragon fears keep one living in the past or the future rather than experiencing life in the present. Fantasy fears can cause us to do a lot of unnecessary running in life, so authority over *dragons* is not a mental game.

But the good news is that God says we will tread on *all* of the powers of the enemy—no matter how loud and bold, sneaky and deceptive, or imaginary those powers might be. God has given us authority over all of them! No longer are we to put up with the paralyzing fears that at one time gripped our hearts and left us powerless at the sight of the evil that was striking all around us. God has given us His *power of attorney*, and these problems now have to submit to the authority of His name. I like that word *tread*. I think of a tank crossing a brushy plain. Where the tank treads go, everything is crushed and left flat on the ground. It is a great picture of our authority over these spiritual enemies as well, treading like a tank and crushing all that is evil in our path. That is a strong description of our authority in walking over the lion, young lion, cobra, and dragon.

Chapter

BECAUSE I LOVE HIM

Because he has loved Me, therefore I will…

—Psalm 91:14

I N VERSES 14–16 OF Psalm 91, the author changes from talking in the third person *about* God's promises to God speaking to us personally from His *secret place* and *announcing* His promises in the first person. It is a dramatic shift in tone, as it moves to God speaking prophetically to each one of us directly, denoting significantly more depth in the relationship.

In these three verses He gives seven promises with as much obvious triumph as a man has when a woman accepts his proposal. A commitment to love involves choice. When you pick one person out of all others, you set your love on that one and embark on a deeper relationship. That is the picture of how God sets His love on us. In the same way, this passage challenges the reader to set his love on God. When he does, the promises come into effect, and God is indulgent with His promises to the one who loves Him.

Love is the cohesiveness that binds man to God, and God will be faithful to His beloved. Love always requires presence and nearness. Special memories are birthed out of relationship. That is why these verses cannot be fully explained but must be experienced. Let me give you an illustration.

If you are a parent, you may have watched in horror as your young child picked up a newly birthed kitten by the throat and carried it all over the yard. You may have wondered how it ever survived.

In our family it was an old red hen that endured the distress dished out by our very enthusiastic children. *Ole Red* would allow herself to be picked up while in the process of laying her egg and would deposit it right in Angie's eager little hands. The children had some merit to what they advertised as *the freshest eggs in town*—a few times the egg never hit the nest. Nesting season had its own special fascination for the children as they watched Ole Red try to hatch out more eggs than she could sit on. The kids would number the eggs in pencil to ensure each egg was properly rotated and kept warm—even rotating eggs between different chickens. They would wait out the twenty-one days and then, with contagious delight, call me out to see the nest swarming with little ones. That old hen had a brood of chicks that was hatched out of eggs from every hen in the henhouse.

Observing a setting hen this close had its own rare charm as one could witness the *protection* she gave those chicks in a way most people never have the chance to observe. I remember her feathers as she fanned them out. I remember the smell of the fresh straw the kids kept in the nest. I remember that I could see through the soft, downy underside and watch the rhythmic beating of her heart. Those chicks had an almost enviable position—something all the books on *the theology of protection* could never explain in mere words. This was the unforgettable picture of a real-life understanding of what it means to be *under the wings*. Those were some happy chicks! *True protection* has everything to do with *closeness*.

Some people acknowledge that there is a God; others *know* Him. Neither maturity nor education or family heritage...or even a lifetime as a nominal Christian can make a person *know* Him. Only an encounter with the Lord and time spent with Him will cause one to lay hold of the promises in Psalm 91.

We need to ask ourselves, "Do I really love Him?" Jesus even asked this of Peter, a close disciple (John 21:15). Can you imagine how Peter must have felt when Jesus asked three times, "Peter, do you love Me?" Even so, we need to question ourselves, because these promises are made only to those who have genuinely set their love on Him. Take special note of the fact that these seven promises are *reserved* for those who return His love.

And remember that the Lord said in John 14:15: "If you love Me, you will keep My commandments." Our obedience is a reliable *telltale* sign that shows we really love Him. Do you love Him? If you do, these promises are for you!

Chapter

GOD IS MY DELIVERER

Because he has loved Me, therefore I will deliver him.
—PSALM 91:14

A PROMISE OF DELIVERANCE IS the first of the seven promises made to the one who loves God. Make it personal! For instance, I quote it like this: "Because I love You, Lord, I thank You for Your promise to deliver me."

When I was young, I personally needed deliverance. I almost destroyed my marriage, my family, and my reputation because I was tormented with fear. One incident opened the door. I can remember the very instant my happy life changed into a nightmare that lasted eight years. And one verse walked me out of this living mental hell: "Whoever calls on the name of the LORD will be delivered" (Joel 2:32)! Many of you desperately need God's promise of deliverance. The Word worked for me, and it will work for you.

There are also other types of deliverances. There is the internal and the external. Ask yourself, "From what is He going to deliver me?"

Remember the external deliverances discussed in previous chapters. God will deliver us from *all* of the following:

- Lion problems
- Young lion problems
- Cobra problems
- Dragon problems
- Terror by night—evils that come through man: war, terror, violence
- Arrows that fly by day—enemy assignments sent to wound
- Pestilence—plagues, deadly diseases, fatal epidemics
- Destruction—evils over which man has no control

In other words, God wants to deliver us from every evil known to mankind. That protection does not stop just because we might be on foreign soil, alone on a dangerous mission, or in the midst of a fierce battle.

It is comforting to know that God involves Himself with the minute details of our lives even when we may be caught off guard. "Lost in the moment" would more adequately describe Justin MacFarland and the team of college students he was leading, along with our daughter, Angelia, as they plunged into the pristine waters of escalating waterfalls deep in the Central American jungles.

After having ministered to the little village at the foot of the mountain in Chiapas for a couple of days, the team decided to make a two-hour hike through the bush up to the fabulous waterfalls before moving on to the next village.

You could hear the falls long before you reached them, so as they approached, the enthusiasm mounted among the college students. As they broke through the foliage to the banks of the river, the group exploded with "wows" and "ooos." In an instant, shoes and socks were shucked and bodies were smashing into the once quiet pools of cool, jungle water. They climbed the falls one tier at a time until they could see the top level.

At the bottom of that top tier is a massive pool of deep, cold water. From the edge of the second level across to the falling water of the top level is about one hundred fifty meters. The hot, muggy air of the jungle drove the college students into the deeper hole, paddling toward the prize of the beautiful top cascade. After gloating in their accomplishment, they dived from the rocks and enjoyed the cool, refreshing pools of water for several hours. With the curiosity of most college boys they had left no stone unturned, and the large group made quite a commotion in their youthful antics.

It was puzzling to some of the group that no locals had accompanied them in their swim across the deep pool to the top of the falls. Justin and the rest of the students, however, had been so energized by the thought of reaching the very top that they hadn't even noticed that their companions had not participated in the swim.

The native children would sporadically clap their hands above their heads, as if they were chomping down into the water towards their peers. The team thought, "Poor kids, we will teach them to swim next year!" A year later when Justin asked why the children did not join in the swim, they were told that huge crocodiles guarded the bigger pools of water. The locals had been quite impressed that the team was brave enough to chance the big pool and its deep water. The students, of course, wanted to know why they had not been warned of the crocodiles. Since they had charged ahead into the water without asking, the locals thought they must know what they were doing. After the initial shock, they realized just how faithful God is and how reliable is His covenant promise to those who believe.

Who knows what dangers actually lurked below the waters of these remote, jungle falls. The locals certainly knew enough not to swim there. When I think of situations like this one that our college students have lived through in their foreign travels, I rejoice to know that God's protection follows us not only into the known but also into the unknown. Like the ignorant enthusiasm of our college group in the jungle, sometimes it is tempting to get caught up in the moment and run ahead of our guide, God's Holy Spirit. Thankfully, God is faithful to offer His covenant protection of Psalm 91 to us even when we may overstep our bounds just a bit. Sometimes, instantly, we know exactly what God has delivered us from. Other times, we find out later, much like this team when they realized they were swimming in a crocodile-infested pool in the jungle. And there will be other things we won't find out about until we get to heaven. How important it is to know beyond a shadow of doubt that our Psalm 91 covenant of protection is absolutely true and reliable—and can deliver us no matter what we may be facing.

Remember that deliverance is all encompassing. It happens within (internal) and without (external); in fact, it surrounds us.

> You are my hiding place; You preserve me from trouble;
> You surround me with songs of deliverance.
> —Psalm 32:7

Angelia has been ministering in the local juvenile prison since she was seventeen years old, and she has experienced God's delivering power on many occasions.

When she first began to minister at the boys' juvenile prison, the volunteer coordinator told Angelia she feared that with her casual attitude, she was going to get stabbed and ruin the program! Angelia laughed at the time and went on to experience years of protection. However, years later as she was leaving the parking lot and heading toward the entrance of the facility, she was thinking about the Monday night lesson, hoping the kids would not be distracted and praying that the message would bear fruit. Giving thought to her safety had never been a priority, and tonight it was definitely the last thing on her mind.

However, at that moment she clearly heard God say, "Trust Me for your protection."

Her response was, "I am!" The incident, however, shocked her out of unconsciously assuming she was immune from danger, not because she consciously held to the promises of God's Word, but because so many years had gone by with no personal danger. She realized she had slipped into coasting rather than trusting. It immediately reminded her how easy it is, over time, to substitute a passive concept of being bullet-proof rather than truly trusting God for His protection. She sensed that this little incident was a spiritual wake-up call, so she began to quote the Bible verses on safety and protection before she entered the facility.

About three weeks later the staff members told her that some of the boys from her dorm were planning to kidnap her and use her as a hostage/shield for their escape! This attempt was thwarted, and later she heard the culprits were put into security lockup. Thankful for the nudge to start getting her faith up, she knew the danger had lifted.

God used this to make her realize that she had quit mixing faith with God's delivering power and that there is no place for this kind of complacency in our walk with God. There is a vast difference between knowing the promises and applying the promises.

God is constantly reminding us that one of His seven bonus promises—if we are trusting Him—is that *He will deliver us!*

Chapter

I AM SEATED ON HIGH

Because he has loved Me...I will set him securely on
high, because he has known My name.

—PSALM 91:14

To be set securely *on high* is the second promise to those who
love the Lord and know Him by name. "It is My name," God
says, "that has been on his lips when he faces troubles, and he
has run to Me. He has called out to Me in faith; therefore, I will set
him on high."

> ...which He brought about in Christ, when He raised Him
> from the dead and seated Him at His right hand in the heav-
> enly places, far above all rule and authority and power and
> dominion, and every name that is named, not only in this age
> but also in the one to come....and raised us up with Him, and
> seated us with Him in the heavenly places in Christ Jesus.
>
> —EPHESIANS 1:20–21; 2:6

It is interesting that God pulls us up to where He is! Things look better from higher up. Our vantage point is much improved, seated with Him on high.

Hebrews 8:11 quotes Jeremiah speaking of the new covenant to come and comparing it to the Old Testament, in effect saying: "They will no longer say, '*Know* [according to *Strong's Concordance*, "to have knowledge of"] the Lord.'" Most people under the Old Testament, according to Jeremiah, only had knowledge *about* God—they just had an *acquaintance* with Him. However, the writer uses a different word *know* in the same verse to describe our knowledge of God under the new covenant.

According to *Strong's Concordance*, the second time the word *know* is used in Hebrews 8:11 means "to stare at, discern clearly, to experience or to gaze with wide open eyes as though gazing at something remarkable." When God refers to our knowing Him today, He is referring to something much more personal than what people experienced during the Old Testament.

It is so important to realize that the name you call on can save you. It can set you securely on high. Or you can use the name and speak evil, which gives no help to your situation. It makes no sense to have access to the name that can work miracles and deliver your life and not use it in a way that renders you mercy. Many times we lose spiritual battles with our mouths, and we open ourselves up for assaults. An environment of cursing opens the door for being cursed; yet calling on God for help renders aid. When you get a revelation of the power of that name, it not only causes you to refrain from evil, but it also gives you a reverence for Him, just as you would respect the name of one of your closest friends. I challenge you to meditate on God's promise: "I will set him on high because he has known My name." These are not just empty words.

This promise of being seated securely on high is for the one who experiences God intimately. Read this verse in first person. "Lord, You have promised You will set me securely on high because I have known Your name on a firsthand basis. I have experienced Your covenant promises described in Your different covenant names."

There is no other name under heaven that has been given among men by which we must be saved [healed, delivered, protected, sustained—according to *Strong's Concordance*].

—Acts 4:12

In the first two sentences alone of Psalm 91, the psalmist refers to God by four different names, progressively denoting stronger relationship. The writer refers to God as the *Most High*, revealing that He is the highest thing that exists. This implies so much more significance when we realize we are set securely on high with the One who is Most High. From on high we have a better vantage point and better perspective. In this opening of Psalm 91, God is also called the *Almighty*, denoting that He is "all" mighty—the most powerful. Next He is referred to as the *Lord*, revealing ownership. Then the psalmist calls Him *my God*, making it personal. We see God unveiled in four unique ways to the man who has known His name.

Verse 14 introduces two conditions and two promises that link back to the beginning of the psalm—because he has loved Me and because he has known My name—each introduced with the word *because* to catch our attention. Then He responds with two promises of deliverance and positioning. We love the fact that God faithfully keeps His promises, but have we kept ours?

Paul was not the only writer who spoke of our being seated on high. Psalm 91 has also made this as a promise to us. Once God seats you on high, you have a new perspective and longing to fulfill your responsibility to the Lord.

Does the position God has raised me to cause me to see things more His way? Am I sloppy and forgetful toward God, or am I more obedient to Him each day? Do I have good follow-through because of my position in Christ, or do I forget all He has done for me? Does the position He has given me reflect that I am seated on high?

Chapter

GOD ANSWERS
MY CALL

He will call upon Me, and I will answer him.
—PSALM 91:15

G OD MAKES A THIRD promise here in verse 15 that He will *answer* those who truly love Him and call on His name. Are we aware of what a wonderful promise God is making to us here?

> This is the confidence which we have before Him, that, if we ask anything according to His will, He hears us. And if we know that He hears us in whatever we ask, we know that we have the requests which we have asked from Him.
> —1 JOHN 5:14–15

Nothing gives me more comfort than to realize that every time I pray in line with God's Word, He hears me. And if He hears me, I know I have the request for which I asked. This one promise keeps me continually searching His Word in order to understand His will and His promises so I can know how to pray more effectively. Sometimes I just cry out to God for help.

During one of our floods several years ago, our twenty-year-old son, Bill, had a herd of goats on some land by the bayou. As the bayou water began to rise and overflow its banks, some men saw Bill's goats being overtaken by the flood and hoisted them up into the loft of a barn to keep them from drowning. By the next morning, the water was like a rushing river—a mile wide—washing away uprooted trees and everything else in its path. Bill had, by this time, been told about his goats, and in spite of the roadblocks and the rapids gushing by, he set out in an old, tin-bottom boat across those swift floodwaters to rescue his little herd of goats. He knew in another few hours they would die from thirst and suffocation.

Of all the herd, little Willie was the most precious because of the time Bill had spent bottle-feeding him. The cry of that little goat was the first Bill heard when he got close to the barn. As you might expect, once Bill forced the loft door open amid the rushing waters, Little Willie was the first to jump into his arms. Then boatload by boatload, goat by goat, Bill got every one of those animals out of the loft and rowed them to safety.

A television camera crew from Abilene, while filming the flood, caught sight of the young boy risking his life to rescue his goats. That became the news story of the day, making the broadcast at six o'clock and again at ten. That is a heartwarming story, but every time I think of Bill rescuing those goats in trouble, I think of how merciful God is to answer us when we sincerely *call to Him* for help.

God is faithful to watch over us using every means possible, but He expects us to be willing to call upon Him. When we call, God is faithful to answer—and sometimes, He uses very unusual means. My mother-in-law, Ruth, became very good friends with Rocky, a three-year-old boxer dog who belonged to her next-door neighbors. She and Rocky would *chat* over the fence that separated their backyards. Whenever Grandmother Ruth was outside, Rocky seemed to know, even if he was inside, and he would bark until someone let him out. One night, shortly after dark, when the couple opened the door, Rocky did not want to come in for the night, which was very unusual. Once he came in, he began to whine and cry, scratching at the front door. When he refused to settle down, his owners finally decided to let him outside, but he kept coming back and whining louder than ever. He absolutely would not stop until he got them to go outside where they were able to hear my eighty-seven-year-old mother-in-law calling for help. She had fallen in her backyard and couldn't get up. It turned out to be a very cold night—one that Ruth might not have survived had she been left on the wet ground all night.

Earlier, when she heard the neighbors close their doors and the dog was in for the night, she said she thought about what a horrible way this was to end up, and she began crying out to the Lord to help her. Because she insisted on living alone, we had been talking to her about always remembering to call on God if she ever got in trouble. She told us that for what seemed like forever, she constantly called out: "Jesus, help me!" She never let up. Over and over in the cold and dark, she cried: "Jesus, help me!" When the neighbors put Rocky in for the night, he just would not settle down, but it was a good while before they finally opened the back door and he was able to bring attention to Mama Ruth. This is a story celebrating not a heroic dog but the power of how God hears when a person cries out to Him. There is no end to God's ways and means of providing protection for those who trust His Word and call upon Him. This is such an important truth for individuals and for families—and for nations.

In the early days of World War II, English soldiers were trapped at Dunkirk—with the German army behind them and the English Channel in front of them. The prime minister warned the nation that no more than twenty or thirty thousand of the two hundred thousand British soldiers could possibly be rescued from those exposed beaches.

But no one could have estimated the power of a nation in prayer. The churches of England were filled...the king and queen knelt at Westminster Abby...the Archbishop of Canterbury...the prime minister...the cabinet...the good Wilhelmina...and all of Parliament were on their knees.

Suddenly, one of the Nazi generals decided to regroup, and he ordered a halt of the German troops when they were only twelve miles away from Dunkirk; Hitler then made a rash decision to hold them there indefinitely. The weather suddenly proved to be a great hindrance to the enemy planes firing on the English, who appeared to be trapped like mice on that French coast. How could that many men be rescued?

Vice Admiral Bertram Ramsay, headquartered in the reinforced tunnels beneath Dover Castle, was put in charge of evacuating the troops. After the first day, fewer than eight thousand troops had been rescued, and the most optimistic estimate was that a total of forty-five thousand might escape before Germany overtook the beaches. In desperation, Ramsay put out a public call for help: everyone with a boat—any kind of boat—was asked to help rescue the troops. Instantly, every imaginable vessel that would float—everything from private boats piloted by bank clerks, fishermen, Boy Scouts, yachtsmen, barge operators, college professors, and tugboat captains started their rescue mission. Even London fire brigade boats got in on the action. Shipyards were quickly set up to repair the damaged vessels so they could return for another load. Anyone would have said the undertaking was absurd, but the *prayers of a nation* strengthened the people in one of the most dangerous and seemingly impossible endeavors in all history.

On the boats taking them to safety, the men began to pray—many had never prayed before. At the camps in England, the men requested permission to pray. It became apparent to all of Britain that their prayers were being heard. By the morning of May 29, officials estimated that 2,000 troops per hour were being evacuated. Nine days after the rescue began, a total of 338,226 people—including about 95,000 French troops—had been rescued.[1]

Not only was the nation of England praying, but also collective prayers were being called for around the world. President Franklin Roosevelt issued a proclamation for prayer, and a nation responded. General Patton issued a call for prayer on the battlefield, and the chaplains and soldiers responded. What tremendous testimonies to the might of the combined prayers of the masses! When we think of the power of individual prayer, let's not forget history's record of what happens by the power of corporate prayer—it strengthens the individual's prayer. When soldiers call upon God—He answers. When nations call upon God—history records it.

GOD RESCUES ME FROM TROUBLE

I will be with him in trouble;
I will rescue him...

—PSALM 91:15

THE FOURTH PROMISE—TO RESCUE *from trouble* those who love the Lord—is found in the middle of verse 15. It is a well-known fact that human nature cries out to God when faced with trouble. Men in prison, soldiers in war, people in accidents—all seem to call out to God when they get in a crisis. Even atheists are known to call on *the God they don't acknowledge* when they are extremely afraid. A lot of criticism has been given to those kinds of *court of last resort* prayers. However, in defense of this kind of praying, we must remember when one is in pain, he usually runs to the one he loves the most and the one he trusts. The alternative is not calling out at all, so this verse acknowledges calling out to God in trouble is a good place for a person to start!

God answers our prayers and rescues us in so many different ways. I am so thankful He is creative and not hindered by our seemingly impossible situations. But we have to ask in faith and not confine Him to our limited resources. God says, "If you love Me, I will be with you when you find yourself in trouble, and I will rescue you." But we have to trust Him to do it *His* way.

> When you pass through the waters, I will be with you;
> And through the rivers, they will not overflow you.
> When you walk through the fire, you will not be scorched,
> Nor will the flame burn you.
>
> —ISAIAH 43:2

Our son, Bill, once saw the *rescuing* power of God when he found himself in serious *trouble* after attempting to swim across a lake that was much wider than he calculated. With no strength left in his body, and having already gone under twice, Bill experienced all the sensations of drowning. But miraculously, God not only provided a woman on the opposite bank, which had been deserted, but also enabled her to throw a life ring (that just *happened* to be near) more than thirty yards, landing within inches of his almost lifeless body. Although some people might call happenings like these a coincidence, the negative situations that we encounter can become *God-incidences* when we trust His Word. That was certainly Bill's *day of trouble*, but I thank God He was with Bill and *rescued* him.

Chapter

GOD HONORS ME

I will... honor him.

—Psalm 91:15

T HE FIFTH PROMISE—TO HONOR those who love God—is in the last part of verse 15. All of us like to be honored. I can remember when the teacher called my name while I was in grade school and complimented my work on a paper I'd turned in. That thrilled me. I was honored.

Several years ago our daughter, Angelia, attended a political rally in our city that was given for George W. Bush when he was campaigning for governor of Texas. She had shared a quick anecdote with him at the beginning of the meeting when they first met. After he had spoken to the group and was leaving with some of his colleagues, everyone was shocked when he left his group and darted back to our daughter to say, "Remember the promise I made—no tears for you in November." (She had told him that she would not be able to hold back the tears if he lost the election.) It honored her that he not only remembered her but also recalled their conversation.

When this book was written, our granddaughter's husband, Heath Adams, was a staff sergeant in the U.S. Air Force. He had recently finished Airman Leadership School and was then stationed at Great Falls, Montana. We were all thrilled when he received the John Levitow Award, the highest award given at the leadership school banquet. It was not only an honor for him, but it was also an honor for his whole squadron. Then he was one of eight people chosen from forty-five hundred security forces to represent Air Force Space Command in the Defender Challenge Competition, where his team took silver medals in the obstacle course and tactics events, placing second overall.

Heath was also a distinguished graduate at Security Force Level II Combat Leaders Course. He won the Air Force SF Noncommissioned Officer Award at 20th Air Force and had the honor of giving a warrior brief to the secretary of the air force—the first warrior brief the secretary had ever heard. The commander coordinated a surprise ceremony to give Heath his promotion and secretly arranged for our granddaughter, Jolena, to be there. Not only was his military service noted, but also his character as a family man, a youth pastor, and, ultimately, a faithful follower of Christ, evidenced in his activity with a local church, was communicated to the group. The ceremony honored Heath before all his peers.

Men have many types of customs to honor other men, from ceremonies and speeches to medals of distinction. I have had the highest admiration for each serviceman I've interviewed as they showed me their Purple Hearts and their Medals of Honor. Those are symbols of the honors that have been bestowed on those recipients.

Not only is it an honor, but it also feels good to have someone we consider important pay special attention to us. However, even though it is a distinct thrill to be honored by man, *how much more of a tribute and a thrill do we experience when God honors us?* Fulfilling our part of the covenant allows God to honor us.

Have you ever thought about what it means to be honored by the

God of the universe? He honors us by calling us His sons and daughters. He honors us by answering when we take His Word seriously and call out to Him in faith. He honors us by recognizing us individually and by preparing a place for us to be with Him eternally. *Giving us honor* is one of the seven unique, bonus promises God made to us in Psalm 91.

Chapter

GOD SATISFIES ME WITH LONG LIFE

With a long life I will satisfy him.

—Psalm 91:16

T HE SIXTH PROMISE OF the final verses of Psalm 91 is found in verse 16. God does not only say He will prolong our lives and give us a lot of birthdays. No! He says He will *satisfy* us with a long life. There are people who would testify that simply having a great many birthdays is not necessarily a blessing. But God says He will give us many birthdays, and as those birthdays roll around, we will experience satisfaction.

It has been said there is a *God-shaped vacuum* inside each of us. Man has tried to fill that vacuum with many different things, but nothing will satisfy the emptiness until it is filled with Jesus. He is the true satisfaction to which God refers in His promise.

God is making the offer. If we will come to Him, let Him fill that empty place on the inside, and allow Him to help us fulfill the call on our lives, then He will give us *a long life* and *satisfy* us as we live it out. Only the dissatisfied person can really appreciate what it means to find satisfaction.

It is a fact that God wants us to live a satisfied life, but let's not neglect the promise of a long life. King David was Israel's most valiant, daring warrior, yet he lived to be a ripe old age—*full of days* as the Old Testament authors liked to say. His life was filled with combat, high-risk situations, and impossible odds. Yet he did not die in battle; his head went down in peace in his old age. Long life is a great concluding promise of protection.

Paul lets us know in Ephesians that we are in a fight. We can't flow with what feels good and win this battle because the enemy will make the wrong path extremely easy to take.

Once, in a boat on the Sea of Galilee the disciples cried out, fearing they would drown in the storm. Jesus, however, had said they must go to the other side. If they had thought through what He had said, they would have known the storm would not harm them because they had His word concerning a mission across the lake. In the same way, if you have been promised a satisfying, long life, then you know you will make it through the present circumstances.

John Evans, a Welsh preacher, told of an incident that happened to his friend during the Civil War soon after he received a captain's commission. Even though many of the men in the army had little regard for religion, it was fashionable for each soldier to carry a Bible.

While following orders to burn a fort, the captain and his men came under very heavy fire from the enemy. When the conflict was over, he found a musket ball had lodged itself in his Bible, which was in his pocket. Had it not been for this intervention, he most assuredly would have been killed. Investigating further, he then discovered that the bullet had come to rest on the verse Ecclesiastes 11:9: "Rejoice, O young man, in thy youth...and walk in the ways of thine heart...but know thou, that for all these things God will bring thee into judgment" (KJV). This message made as deep an impression on his mind as did the way it was delivered. As a nonreligious man, he realized the Bible had literally done more than just attempt to save his soul. As a result, he immediately turned his heart toward God and continued to be devout in his Christian walk to a good, old age. He often testified how the Bible became, that day, the salvation of his body as well as his soul.[1]

God was not interested only in protecting and extending this man's life—He was more interested in his faithful obedience as he lived out that life. In the same way, God wants us to claim the promise of long life, but He also wants us to use our long life living for Him. Ask yourself, "What *am* I going to do with my long life?"

Chapter

21

I BEHOLD HIS SALVATION

...and let him see *My salvation.*
—Psalm 91:16, emphasis added

ALLOWING THOSE WHO LOVE Him to *see His salvation* is the seventh promise in Psalm 91, found in the last part of verse 16. God wants us to take hold of His salvation.

The movement of this last line in Psalm 91 describes our ultimate, final victory. The order of this sentence gives us the promise that we will see salvation face-to-face *during* and *after* our *long, satisfied life.* This moves us beyond an intellectual knowledge of salvation all the way to relationship. It secures our future, but it starts now. Jesus constantly reminded us, "Salvation is now! Today it has come!" Many people are surprised when they look up the word *salvation* in a Bible concordance and find it has a much deeper meaning than just a ticket to heaven. We often miss the richness of this promise.

According to *Strong's Concordance*, the word *salvation* includes health, healing, rescue, deliverance, safety, protection, and provision. What more could we ask? God promises He will allow us to see and *take hold of* His health, His healing, His deliverance, His protection, and His provision!

Many people read Psalm 91 and simply see it with their eyes, but very few *behold* it in their lives. My prayer is for that to change. One of my biggest thrills comes when people write or call after I've taught this truth, and they describe the ecstatic joy of having it come alive in their heart. I love to hear the extent to which they have actually *taken hold of* this covenant and started experiencing it as a vital part of their existence.

You can be in the midst of a situation where the enemy is all around and still behold the salvation of the Lord. Many have actually experienced the sensation of the presence of the Lord in the midst of chaos. In the testimonies that follow in the next section of this book, your heart will be encouraged by those who have beheld firsthand the salvation of the Lord. Read their stories in their own words. The truth about God's salvation—His protection, deliverance, health, and provision—is more than just wishful thinking. It is a *promise* of which one can actually *take hold*.

SUMMARY

NOTHING IN THIS WORLD is more reliable than God's promises—when we believe them, refuse to waver, and make His Word *our final authority* for every area of life.

There is, however, a uniqueness about this psalm. Promises of protection can be found throughout the Bible, but Psalm 91 is the only place in the Word where all of the protection promises are brought together in one collection—forming a covenant written through the Holy Spirit. How powerful that is!

I believe Psalm 91 is a covenant—a spiritual contract that God has made available to His children. It is desperately needed in these difficult days. There are some who sincerely ask, "How do you know you can take a *song* from the psalms and base your life on it?" Jesus answered that question. The value of the psalms was emphasized when He cited them as a source of truth that must be fulfilled:

> Now He said to them, "These are My words which I spoke to you while I was still with you, that all things which are written about Me in the Law of Moses and the Prophets *and the Psalms* must be fulfilled.
>
> —LUKE 24:44, EMPHASIS ADDED

When Jesus specifically equates the Psalms to the Law of Moses and the Prophets, we see that it is historically relevant, prophetically sound, and totally applicable and reliable.

At a time when there are so many uncertainties facing us, it is more than comforting to realize that God not only knows ahead of time what we will be facing but also makes absolute provision for us.

Someone once pointed out, "It is interesting that the world must have gotten its distress 911 number from God's answer to our distress call—Psalm 91:1."

It seems only a dream now to think back to the time when my mind was reeling in fears and doubts. Little did I know when I asked God that pertinent question—"Is there any way for a Christian to escape all the evils that are coming on this world?"—He was going to give me a dream that would not only change my life but also change the lives of thousands of others who would hear and believe.

WHAT MUST I DO TO BE SAVED?

W E'VE TALKED ABOUT PHYSICAL protection. Now let's make sure you have eternal protection. The promises from God in this book are for God's children who love Him. If you have never given your life to Jesus and accepted Him as your Lord and Savior, there is no better time than right now.

There is none righteous, not even one.

—ROMANS 3:10

For all have sinned and fall short of the glory of God.

—ROMANS 3:23

But God demonstrates His own love toward us, in that while we were yet sinners, Christ died for us.

—ROMANS 5:8

For God so loved the world [you], that He gave His only begotten Son, that whoever believes in Him shall not perish, but have eternal life.

—JOHN 3:16

There is nothing we can do to earn our salvation or to make ourselves good enough to go to heaven. It is a free gift!

> For the wages of sin is death, but the *free* gift of God is eternal life in Christ Jesus our Lord.
> —ROMANS 6:23, EMPHASIS ADDED

There is also no other avenue through which we can reach heaven other than Jesus Christ—God's Son.

> And there is salvation in no one else; for there is no other name under heaven that has been given among men by which we must be saved.
> —ACTS 4:12

> Jesus said to him, "I am the way, and the truth, and the life; no one comes to the Father but through Me."
> —JOHN 14:6

You must believe that Jesus is the Son of God, that He died on the cross for your sins, and that He rose again on the third day.

> ...who [Jesus] was declared the Son of God with power by the resurrection from the dead.
> —ROMANS 1:4

You may be thinking, "How do I accept Jesus and become His child?" God in His love has made it so easy.

> If you confess with your mouth Jesus as Lord, and believe in your heart that God raised Him from the dead, you will be saved.
> —ROMANS 10:9

But as many as received Him, to them He gave the right to become children of God, even to those who believe in His name.

—John 1:12

It is as simple as praying a prayer similar to this one—if you sincerely mean it in your heart:

Dear God:

I believe You gave your Son, Jesus, to die for me. I believe He shed His blood to pay for my sins and that You raised Him from the dead so I can be Your child and live with You eternally in heaven. I am asking Jesus to come into my heart right now and save me. I confess Him as the Lord and Master of my life.

I thank You, dear Lord, for loving me enough to lay down Your life for me. Take my life now and use it for Your glory. I ask for all that You have promised for me.

In Jesus's name, amen.

STORIES THAT DEMAND TO BE TOLD—
PSALM 91 TESTIMONIES

JOHN AND VIRGINIA LOYD

A few weeks prior to Ivan, Hurricane Francis looked like it was threatening Orange Beach. Virginia called Jack Ruth for prayer, and he said that Francis would pass us by (it did), but that he was worried about the next one, which turned out to be Ivan. As we watched Ivan take its turn north directly toward us, Virginia asked God to replace the thoughts of fear that were tormenting her. God told her to "have a faith picture of everything just as it was before Ivan." This allowed her to exchange fear thoughts with God's promises in Psalm 91!

After Ivan made landfall six miles west of us, putting Orange Beach on the *dirty* side of the storm, we had to wait three days until we were allowed back into Orange Beach. The city was under martial law with fully armed National Guard units posted at roadblocks everywhere. They would not allow us to go to our house. Supernaturally, God directed me to go to City Hall, where I saw a pile of passes on a desk. I asked a friend who worked there what they were, and she told me they were contractor's passes, and I could buy one for $50. I bought three, and we had unrestricted access to all areas of the city.

Jack had told us that the storm would pass over us. Little did we know that God meant literally pass *over* us. The roof of our back porch, weighing at least a ton, was lifted off and was hurled OVER our house without touching a thing. It ended up in our side yard.

The water had risen to within six feet of our house, and you could clearly see a high-water mark all around our house, yet no water got to us.

The big remaining issue was our condo on the beach. From pictures we had seen on TV prior to coming back to Orange Beach, we knew things were bad. We knew the roof of the condo directly over us was gone. When we drove past our condo, it was awful. The roof was off the building over the unit directly above us, and that unit already had a red *condemned* sticker on the door. We decided not to deal with the condo the first day. The next day I left Virginia at a restaurant with friends and set out to pick up some supplies we had left in the driveway of a friend's house. On the way I had to drive by the condo. I asked myself, "What kind of a man am I that I can't face this?" So I parked the car and went up to the condo. When I opened the door, I could hardly contain my emotions. I just started shouting with joy! Everything was exactly as we had left it! There was absolutely no damage to anything—no water, no nothing. It was as though we had just gone to the store and come back to our beautiful condo. The unit directly above us was completely destroyed. There was no roof, and it was total devastation. Yet we were spared, just as God had told Virginia we would be.

At the time of the storm, we had a sales contract on the condo for $625,000, which fell through because the buyer's condo was destroyed by the storm and she couldn't go through with the contract. We had already bought our house and really needed to sell the condo, so we seemed to be stuck. Then God provided a developer who wanted to tear down our condo building to build a high-rise condo. In June, we closed on that deal at a price of $920,000, with no closing costs or broker's fees! God had answered our prayers and given us $300,000 more than we were asking! Sadly, many of our neighbors decided to stay in a deal with the developer for a new condo in the high-rise that he proposed to build. In September, however, Hurricane Katrina hit the Gulf Coast, and property values literally fell through the floor overnight. The developer went bankrupt, and the project was canceled. Those neighbors who had stayed in the deal lost everything.

On September 16, 2010, it will be six years after Ivan hit. The devastation is still evident around us, but *it has not come near our dwelling place.* Today, 40 percent of the condos and houses that were on the beach in Gulf Shores and Orange Beach are simply gone. We have watched friends be assessed $100,000 to rebuild their condos that were not completely destroyed. We are awed and humbled that the Loyd home is still full of the life that Jesus Christ has made possible through Psalm 91.

AUTHOR'S ADDITION TO THE LOYD'S MIRACLE

A year after Hurricane Ivan hit, Jack and I stayed in the beach home (that God had spared) of our friends, John and Virginia Loyd in Orange Beach, Alabama. For one week we just drove through the area, appalled at the devastation we saw—even after that many months of repairs had taken place. A stone's throw from their house, all the decking at the public boat docks, the gigantic dry dock building, and the glass in a restaurant had all been blown away. When the storm was over, what was left of the marina building was under three feet of water. On the other side of the house we saw what once was a shopping center, which had been reduced to a pile of rubble. Condos and hotels were completely gutted. Even after that length of time, mounds of siding and roofing shingles from the homes next to our friends' beach home still littered the adjacent properties. Only after seeing the destruction with our own eyes did we realize the supernatural protection the Loyds had received. Prior to and during the hurricane, they had called us often, stating their total trust in the Lord's Psalm 91 covenant promise of protection and getting us to join in faith with them. When they returned to the area, with the exception of the back porch, there was no damage to their beach house or their condo. In spite of the fact that the condo was directly on the ocean, when John opened the door to the condo, not even a picture on the wall had been disturbed, nor was the patio glass door broken (NOT covered with plywood). Yet the eye of Hurricane

Ivan had gone directly over the top of their building. When a hurricane passes over, flooding brings much of the destruction because the water goes everywhere. Only God knows how He kept the water out of their beach home! *The Word works!* Coincidence? If you had driven down Beach Road (even a year later, when we did), you would know that it was nothing but the power of God that protected them. Praise God! Psalm 91 is not limited to areas where hurricanes can't reach. We can even be immune in the midst of mass destruction. "You will only look on with your eyes and see the recompense of the wicked" (Ps. 91:8).

MICHELE HARGROVE

I live in Houston, Texas, and am the mother of three. A friend of mine had given me your book in my Bible study, and we all read it and loved it. To have it always handy, I had specifically downloaded it on an iPhone application. While on vacation skiing, I decided to use the extra time on the lifts to use my phone and go over the Scripture. Then, while on the slopes, I'd try to pray it aloud to help me memorize it.

Ross with his sisters Emily and Kara

Our kids are a little older (nineteen, fifteen, and twelve), so they enjoyed skiing this trip without us. It was on the sixth day that I just happened to look up on a slope and saw the three of them going up a lift. We got their attention and then all met at the top. After visiting for a while, we made plans to meet up later for lunch, and all took off down the mountain (my husband and I together and the kids all together). About halfway down the mountain I came upon my husband in the middle of the slope, hollering, and there was all kinds of commotion going on. My son lay crumpled at the base of a tree.

Ross shortly after the accident

He was hit by a huge man (at least 200 pounds) who was going full blast down the mountain and ran into my son. Ross is a small kid for his age. He weighs around 75 pounds soaking wet! My husband saw the impact and saw the man hit him, then *helicopter* through the air and hit a tree! The man was standing when I came up, but only seconds later he went unconscious. If you have never skied, the speed that you can get up heading down a mountain at full blast can do a great deal of damage. As my husband and I came upon our son, he tried to sit up, and his arm was dangling in a very sickening and unnatural position. When paramedics arrived, I backed away and took my two daughters by the hand, and we prayed Psalm 91 out loud over Ross. After they loaded him behind a sled, I was able to ride the snowmobile that dragged him down the hill.

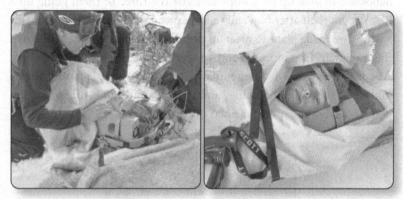

A rescue worker comforts Ross as he is being prepared for transport down the mountain

I prayed this psalm continuously, over and over, as we headed for the ambulance. Not only was I worried about the arm, but also there was concern for neck and head injuries as well. We were rushed to the hospital, and after X-rays and CAT scans were done on him, we were given his condition—not a bone broken, not a thing wrong with him! He was released, and although he was sore and a little bruised, he was fine. My husband and I both insisted on further tests for his arm because we had both seen it dangling and just knew it had to be broken. But God answered our prayer and healed him completely! I feel it was a miracle that we just happened to see them on that huge mountain with tons of lifts. It was a blessing that we were there with them and could help them all cope through such a horrific ordeal. It was a miracle that my tiny son came out fine while this huge man ended up with many problems and a long stay in the hospital.

Thank you so much for writing this book. Who knows what would have happened if I had never read of powerful Psalm 91! My son is only twelve, but he has a powerful testimony that he can now use to help people understand the love of God and the power of prayer and God's covenant promise. God is so good!

NORM AND EVALYN SCHULZ

It was the day before Thanksgiving, and my husband, Norm, said he would pick me up at the State Line Airport. We were excited about the trip, as we were going to have Thanksgiving dinner with our daughter, Pamela, and her husband, Hal, and our first grandbaby, Cinnamon. Norm was a pilot and kept the plane in an east Kansas City airport. I arrived at the State Line Airport and started to wait.

Previously I had memorized the Ninety-first Psalm after receiving a track with the psalm on one side and a testimony on the back. The testimony was about a British regiment that served in World War II for more then four years without losing a man. This unparalleled record was made possible by means of the active cooperation of officers and men in memorizing and repeating regularly the words of the Ninety-first Psalm, which has been called *the psalm of protection*. This testimony was such an encouragement that I needed to commit the psalm to memory. How blessed I have been for having it in my heart!

That morning at the airport I had a foreboding spirit. After waiting in the State Line Airport for some time, the feeling increased. Finally Norm called the airport, and I found I was at the wrong airport. He was planning to pick me up at the Olathe Airport. He told me to sit tight, and he would be there soon to pick me up.

When he arrived, he didn't shut the engine off as there had been a problem getting it started. This didn't exactly help my uneasiness, but we took off and were on our way. I started to pray, and, as was my custom when flying in our little plane, I was praying the Ninety-first Psalm. Before leaving the east Kansas City airport, Norm had made a phone call to our daughter and had left his billfold at the airport when he called. Norm had told me that since it was getting late, we wouldn't bother with trying to get it.

We were in the air only a few minutes when I sensed the plane losing altitude. I asked Norm if something was wrong, and he said, "No, I just decided to go back to the Kansas City Airport to pick up my bill-fold." That was a relief, but I kept praying the Ninety-first Psalm. Norm called the people where he kept the plane to tell them he was coming back, so, as we touched down, one of the men came running out with his billfold. "At last," I thought, "well, now we are off. OK!" But not quite! As we were going down the runway within seconds of being in the air, suddenly the airplane started shaking, and smoke and flames were shooting out in front of us. Norm pulled the throttle wire completely out. I threw my hands up in the air and shouted, "Praise God!" Then, as soon as the shaking began to subside, we jumped out of the plane. The people at the airport came running out and began working to put out the fire. We found that the propeller had broken in half and had flown about a block away where children had been playing in the yard only minutes before.

Back at the airport we were trying to decide what to do. Norm was sure I would never fly again. Just then, our other airplane, which had been rented, returned. By this time it was getting dark, and I didn't especially like to fly at night, but when Norm asked me what I wanted to do, I said, "If God had to go through all of this to keep us safe, I am ready to fly." I was thinking about my going to the wrong airport, Norm's change of mind to go pick up his billfold, and the accident happening on the ground instead of in the air. My heart was so thankful that God had spared our lives.

What an encouragement for us to "dwell in the secret place of the

Most High and trust in Him." There have been other many less spectacular times when God has allowed me to pray with numerous people in hospitals. One such time was with my mother-in-law, right before she had a mastectomy. As I prayed the Ninety-first Psalm, we felt the presence of God and the peace He gave her at the age of ninety-one. After that, she lived to the age of ninety-seven. To God be the glory!

LOUISETTE BIRON

This is my testimony of God's goodness. I decided to clean out our walk-in closet. To reach the top shelves, I had to stretch high above my head, and my hand accidentally pulled down guns that I did not know were loaded. One of the guns fell and hit the floor, causing it to go off. I was startled and could not find where the bullet had ended up. I told my son, and he too was puzzled where the bullet had gone. After he left for work, I continued to remove everything that was on the top shelf. While doing that, I discovered that the bullet went behind a pile of hats. Then a few hours later I discovered, to my surprise, that the bullet had gone through my left pant leg, through two walls and ended up in the ceiling. Realizing the bullet had come close enough to my leg to go through my pant leg without touching my skin, I felt so very blessed. God had spared my life big-time,

Place where bullet went through pant leg after gun went off

and I knew it was because of my Psalm 91 covenant of protection. I realized how easily I could have been injured or killed apart from God's protection. I know it was a miracle of God. I have had Psalm 91 hanging on my wall for the last seventeen years, and I firmly believe in His protection. He loves and protects me, and I give Him the glory. I read your book and I loved it.

Author's Note: Louisette Biron was born twenty-five miles from Quebec City, Quebec, Canada, in 1943. She married her husband, John, a successful entrepreneur in 1967. They moved permanently to the United States in 1976, where they owned a successful Laundromat, which they later sold. They became U.S. citizens in 2006. Born again in May of 1992, Louisette was delivered from smoking five months later. After trying for seven years against all odds, John and Louisette had a miracle baby, Nelson. Two years after selling their business, Louisette was employed at a health food store, where she joyfully shared her faith in Jesus until the store closed in 2008. Her husband passed to heaven in 2009. She currently resides in Clermont, Florida.

TAYLOR BALL
by Cathi Ball

Just nineteen days before one of the devastating fires in Texas, Taylor Ball had won the Texas Cattle Raisers award for stewardship of his ranch. The ranch was beautiful, and the grass was tall. Taylor had created twenty-two water tanks, some of which were later used by helicopters to refill their tanks to put out the fires. Cathi Ball, Taylor's mom, had recently listened to "Psalm 91" by Peggy Joyce Ruth as Peggy Joyce explained all the protection that God provides. Cathi said, "If there was ever a day when I understood that God could protect us from anything, it was that day. I started praying and reading His words of protection over us back to Him, reminding God of His promises."

The fire burned several thousand acres and destroyed miles of fence. But it harmed nothing of Taylor's that was not easily replaceable.

You can see where the fire burned up to the rail fence of Taylor's ranch.

Taylor called shortly after the fire passed. The fire had burned around his house—stopping right at the rail fence surrounding his yard. He  could hardly believe it! The fire also burned around his shop and barn. It also burned around his hay bales. In addition, it left two wheat fields, which was enough feed for his cattle to eat until the grass grew back. It did not hurt any of his cattle, horses, or dogs. The fire also burned around his hunting cabin. What a mighty God we serve!

Cathi Ball

ELAINE BONAIRE

It was early in the summer of 1999 that I first learned about praying Psalm 91. I started praying it every day. That fall, after leaves were pretty much covering the ground here at the cottage that my grampa built, a ground fire started outdoors. On a Saturday afternoon, I was washing my hair after a haircut. After stopping my hair dryer, I heard an airplane. That is not unusual, as we are in the flight path to the airport. I noticed that the airplane didn't seem to be going away and concluded that for some reason it must be circling. About then a neighbor from down at the bend in the road was knocking at the door. He told me there was a fire outside and that the fire department had already been called. I had not noticed any fire or smoke a short while earlier when I arrived back from my haircut, so it must have just gotten started.

I put my shoes on and went outdoors. There was a brisk wind blowing uphill off of our small, inland Michigan lake, but the fire was still burning dry leaves as it moved down the hill toward the lake. On the opposite side of the hill, the wind was pushing the fire in the other direction. It jumped the sandy, two-track road. There are lots of trees around here.

I started raking leaves away from the tent on my neighbor's property next door. Our neighbor raked leaves away from the woodshed on the next property beyond hers. The owners were gone. Before long, the fire department, police, and DNR vehicles converged on the area and put the fire out. It was mainly a ground fire. Sadly, a storage shed on the property next door burned up. Some trees were affected to a greater height, but most trees in the burned area didn't show black up very far. The fire came within one foot of the front corner of our cottage, but stopped without doing any damage. Parked side by side, parallel to our cottage, were my car, my brother's utility trailer, his motorboat, and the cottage sailboat. *The fire did not come anywhere near them.* When the fire jumped the road, it didn't even reach our outhouse, which we haven't needed for years.

... no disaster will come near your tent.

—PSALM 91:10, NIV

I am convinced it was because of praying Psalm 91 every day that summer before the fire that the cottage, car, trailer, boats, and even the outhouse were spared. And even though the flames got pretty high, and the neighbor's shed burned, the trees did not catch fire and spread further. There are lots of trees surrounding the lake, and many are pine. It was an added blessing that it was a daytime fire.

PEYTON ADAMS AND
HER MOM, JOLENA

I am a busy mom of three, so I am often in a hurry to get somewhere. On this particular day I was rushing out the door to take photos for a friend.

My husband was in the garage with the garage door up. He and one of his friends, Matt, were talking and looking at guy stuff. They had come home during a break from a church men's conference, and they only had an hour to spare before they had to be back. As they were gathering up what they needed for shooting skeet at one of the events, they were caught up in their plans for this exciting part of the weekend conference.

I had told our three children—ages seven, five, and three—to stay inside the house and play and that I would be right back; if they needed something, their daddy was in the garage. So I jumped in the car, put it in reverse, and suddenly remembered I forgot the address of the friend's house where I was to take the photos. I ran back into the house, rummaged through a bag, found the address, and then I was off once again.

None of my children were in sight, but I could hear the noise of their playing. I yelled good-bye one more time, took a quick look at my watch, and raced back to my van. Before I backed up, I opened up the piece of paper with the address on it and started thinking about where I needed to go. Since we live on a military base, I have had to learn the layout of the city each time my husband has been transferred during the last ten years. Having formulated a map in my head, I put the car in reverse and started backing. In a big hurry to make best use of the hour that Heath was giving me, I tuned out the rest of the world. The children would not even know I had left, and I would be back before they missed me. I had told them to stay inside—and their daddy was there if they needed him. The kids couldn't get into too much trouble upstairs before I could be back home, but just as a precaution, I would hurry back as quickly as I could.

This is the exact moment that the miracle happened: my minivan window was up, my mind was focused on what I had to do, and any anxiety was being quieted inside of me because I had left my children safely upstairs. With that assurance, I hurriedly pulled out of the driveway. But who knew that *one second* would have made all the tragic, heart-crushing difference in the world. And that is the difference the Word makes.

Suddenly, I heard someone shout. Who had yelled? I slammed on the brakes and looked up. My husband's friend, Matt, had yelled at me to stop! He and my husband were running toward the van, hollering Peyton's name! I got out of the car and, to my absolute horror, realized that in the midst of all of that, my daughter had run outside, climbed on her bike, and driven it behind my van. As I had backed out, she was knocked over and, leaning over on her bike, was holding on to the bumper.

Matt was trying to get me to hear him over the noise of the engine as he lurched forward. You can imagine the agony of our five-year-old child as she clung for her very life to the bumper that was backing over her.

I never saw her behind me. Even though I was looking back over my shoulder rather than trusting my rearview mirror, she was too far below the back window to be noticed. It is pointless to say that there is a major blind spot in a minivan. She had ridden behind my van while I was looking down at that address. By the time I stopped, it was too late—she had been thrown down under the back of the minivan. In what was measured by seconds, but is a parent's eternity and anguish beyond words, neither I nor Heath nor Matt knew what to expect as we ran for the back of the van. She was lying on the ground under the back of our van, with her head in direct line of the rear tire. The bike was under the car tire, totally demolished, and Peyton was under her fallen bike. One second more and life as we knew it would have ended forever.

Her bicycle was crunched beyond any future use. As I picked her up off of the ground, I was praying and checking her out all in one movement to see if she had been harmed in any way!

She calmly looked at me—*the driver who, seconds before, had not seen her behind the minivan hanging on for dear life as I gassed it.* She said, "It's OK, Mom, I'm not hurt, but I think I'm going to need a new bike." And truly, there was not a scratch on her! I held her and gave thanks and praise to God. I couldn't see my daughter, but God sees everything, and He put someone there to see her and yell at me just in time! God had Matt there the day we needed him.

Immediate evaluation of how she had gotten herself in this predicament left us knowing that Peyton had broken some rules—going outside when I, her mom, had told her to stay inside and forgetting that I had told her to never ride her bike around someone in a car. However, Peyton's only horror was that the bike was demolished. Even to this day—whenever this story is retold—Peyton only speaks of the tragedy of how badly the bike was crushed. What is mind-boggling is this— how did the van crush the bike beyond repair, knock down the child, throwing her beneath the van, yet she is pulled out without a scratch on her? There are some *hows* that have not been answered, but I definitely know *who* protected her.

Heath and Jolena Adams with Peyton and her brothers.

I am a mom who prays Psalm 91 word for word over my family—weekly, pulling out the covenant and saying it aloud. Daily I pray for my family's protection and remind myself of the angelic shield around them. I had prayed preventively that my children would never be harmed, specifically by cars or bicycle wrecks. Psalm 91 has been the promise that my husband and I have stood on for our children all of their lives, and we certainly know that God truly heard our prayers that day.

JAMES AND CULLEN

Author's Note: I am going to let James Zintgraff tell this next miracle in his own words of how God used him to spare my grandson's life.

The summer that Cullen was five years old, I was swimming with him and his cousins in their pool. One of the adults had said, "OK, everyone out of the pool." Everyone else had headed inside the house, when Cullen saw a plastic life raft come floating by. He said, "Hey, James, watch this," as he stepped off the side of the pool onto the raft like it was a solid piece. It flipped out from under him, and he fell backward into the water, grazing his head on the side of the pool as he fell.

It was the deep end of the pool, and I watched Cullen, with his arms and legs outstretched, just start sinking to the bottom. I dove in and grabbed him under the arms, but he is unusually big for his age and weighed more than I did. His dad always said that he felt like a chunk of lead when you tried to lift him, so I wondered if I could get him to the top of the water—especially since he must have been dazed from scraping his head on the concrete.

I knew we were in trouble, so I called on God, and suddenly, I felt someone grab me from behind and begin pushing Cullen and me straight up from the bottom of the pool. (I thought one of the adults had seen us and dove in to help me.) I shot up out of the water with Cullen above me. Then it was like someone pulled Cullen from my arms and laid him on the side of the pool. (I was in water way over my head, so there was no way I could have lifted deadweight out of the pool.) Cullen started crying and coughing, and when I looked around, no one was there—absolutely no one! I knew God had heard me call, and He had sent an angel to answer my call, just like He promises in Psalm 91.

By this time the adults came running out of the house to see if we were OK. They treated me like a hero, and I was given a plaque that says, "James Zintgraff saved Cullen Ruth's life," but I knew that I could not have done that rescue alone. I was only an eleven-year-old kid. I know that God heard me and sent His angel to answer my call.

JULEE SHERRICK PATTI

It was 7:00 a.m. on a gorgeous Sunday morning in Fort Worth, Texas. I had awakened early to make strawberry Bavarian pies for an after-church covered-dish dinner. Just as two beautiful pies had finished baking, I heard a knock at the door. Never dreaming anything horrible would happen at seven in the morning, I opened the door. After all, the day before, someone in my apartment complex had stopped by looking for their lost cat, and another stopped by selling Girl Scout cookies. I opened the door about three inches, when the man outside the door forced his way into my apartment. I immediately started screaming, "No! No! No!" It did not take long to realize that his intention was rape. I also remember thinking, "Things like this don't happen to me. I must be dreaming." He pushed me into my bedroom, which was to the left of my front door, and onto the bed. We wrestled on the bed for what seemed to be approximately ten minutes. I remember thinking, "My God cares about everything that goes on in our lives, and I know He is going to deliver me. I just don't know how." My emotions were hysterical, but my spirit was strong. I repeatedly said, "Jesus, help me; Jesus, help me." The man told me to shut up numerous times. I answered back, "I don't know who you are or what you have done, or even if the police are after you, but you need Jesus. I am going to church today, and you can come."

He seemed to snap out of his stupor momentarily. I could smell alcohol on his breath. He looked over at a picture I had on a nightstand next to my bed and said, "Is that a picture of you and your dad?"

I said, "Yes; what about your dad?"

He replied, "You don't even want to know." It was evident that his home life was abusive or dysfunctional at best. I repeated that he needed Jesus. I could see his eyes begin to dilate, and a demonic look came over his face as he started after me again. I began to scream out, "Jesus, Jesus!"

He said, "Shut up, if you want to live!" I knew his intention was rape, but the thought of him trying to kill me had not yet entered my mind. My mind began to race as my life flashed before my eyes. Somehow I got away and slipped out into the living room of my small apartment. He followed swiftly and took hold of my wrists, as we landed in a sitting position facing each other on the couch. I looked at him and said, "I want you to know that there are angels in this room!"

He replied, "There are demons in this room too."

I said, "Well, my angels are stronger than your demons!" It was as if he had no power after that statement. His hands that had once clinched my wrists dropped, and he let me go.

He then asked promptly, "Where is the kitchen?" I kept thinking to myself, "What does he want in the kitchen?" He said that he wanted a glass of water, and he proceeded into the kitchen to get one. I was standing in the living room area approximately thirteen feet away from him.

I lifted up my hands and started to praise God. I said, "Lord, I thank You for my life, and I thank You for his life."

He looked at me and said, "You thank God for my life?"

I said, "Yes, I thank Him for your life too." I started thanking God again: "I thank You, Lord, for all that You have done for me. I praise You because of who You are." I thanked God and praised Him for everything I could think of at that moment. Then I paused, looked at him, and firmly said, "Would you leave now?" When I said those words, he looked at me strangely, and I immediately ran for the door. I did not realize that he had locked the door when he came in. So I pulled the door and quickly tried to unlock the dead bolt. By that time he was on my heels. The lock sprang back as if an angel was helping me. I felt the air move as he lunged for me. Already through the door, my heart beating, I ran, desperately looking for anyone who could help me. As I was running away, I glanced back to see if he was following me. When he departed my apartment door, he turned to the right into the inner court of the apartment complex so no one would see him chasing me. I had turned left into the parking lot for help.

Because it was early on a Sunday morning, there was hardly anyone outside in this large apartment complex. I found one man who was delivering papers. In my white terrycloth bathrobe and slippers, I went up to him and told him what had just happened. I asked if he would stay with me until the police came, and he agreed. I called the police from a pay phone, and they arrived in approximately five minutes.

The police filed a report of all the details. They took fingerprints off the doorway, the kitchen, and off the cup from which he drank. The only fingerprints that they retrieved of any value were the ones on the cup. The police explained to me that I was one lucky girl. They said that it was unheard of for a man with the intent of rape to be in my apartment for more than twenty-five minutes, and yet I would end up unharmed and not raped. I told them that God had delivered me and that I was so grateful. They said, "You sure had something working for you!" With just a couple of bruises on my body, and the back of his earring left behind, I knew God had delivered me from that horrifying situation on that early Sunday morning. I called my parents at the church where they pastor in New Jersey to explain what had happened. They knew something was wrong to get an emergency call from me in the middle of a church service. My mother was in tears as she told me how she had been up all night praying the night before. Her spirit was troubled, and she knew something was not right. Thank God for godly parents, parents who know how to pray and are yielded to the Holy Spirit.

I called my pastors where I attended church in Fort Worth to let them know why I was not in church and why my strawberry Bavarian pies were not going to make it to the covered-dish dinner. They were supportive, kind, and asked me if they could do anything to help. I assured them I was fine and asked them to keep praying for me.

After the police had gone and I was alone, I thanked God over and over. I told Him: "I will never be ashamed of You before people again. You delivered me, and I will proclaim Jesus to people and not be afraid of what anyone thinks. I will never be ashamed of You again!" I have had many opportunities to share this story of God's miraculous protection and deliverance. I truly believe that when I said, "My angels are stronger than your demons," the angels were empowered by my words to receive strength from on high to defeat any demonic forces that were controlling that man. I believe that when I lifted my hands and started praising God, *praise*, one of the weapons we have been given as Christians, launched a missile from heaven and confused the enemy's camp. I understand what it means to have Psalm 91:11 hold true: "For He will give His angels charge concerning you, to guard you in all your ways."

The man who was convicted of this crime had been convicted many times prior to this offense. He had also been convicted for robbery, battery, and assault. The Fort Worth police could not believe that he was in my apartment for that length of time and that I was able to escape unharmed and not sexually assaulted. By the power of God, I came out of that situation with only a couple of bruises and scrapes. Praise God for divine angelic intervention.

KAREN PICKETT

Several months ago while browsing in the Christian bookstore, I was drawn to a book called *Psalm 91: God's Shield of Protection*, written by an author unknown to me—some lady with three first names (Peggy Joyce Ruth). I was searching for something else, so I walked away, but the Holy Spirit seemed to keep drawing my attention back to that book. I resisted—I always buy more books than I can possibly read—but sure enough, that book came home with me.

Several weeks later, the *Psalm 91* book made its way to the top of my reading stack. As I read the book, the promises contained in this chapter of Scripture stirred my heart, and I was sorry I had not picked it up sooner. My spirit immediately grasped the importance and the timeliness of this message. The more I read, the more God's covenant promise of protection thrilled me in an entirely new way. The Holy Spirit's calling me to purchase this book was no doubt an invitation to a divine appointment with God. Reading and pondering, my spirit digested every verse and every promise of Psalm 91. Because I firmly believe that the covenant promises in Psalm 91 can keep us safe in the days to come, I purchased a book for each of my children and each of the intercessors who pray for our ministry. Those who have already received their books were excited to learn more about God's offer of covering for those who truly dwell in the secret place of the Most High God. Having received new revelation of God's Psalm 91 protection over me, I gained a deeper understanding of how I activate His promise. I spent much time searching my heart to be sure that I was indeed dwelling in that secret place. I became more aware of a new peace in my spirit, and I had a heightened awareness of the protection under which I walked. Little did I know how quickly the Lord would confirm His promise to me.

Last Tuesday evening I drove myself to a missions base where we minister, located a few miles outside of town on a secondary two-lane highway. The road was wet and the weather was rainy and foggy, so I was driving very cautiously. Heavy traffic was coming toward me, but only two other cars were going my direction, one car in front of me and another one some distance behind me. I prayed as I drove, remaining peacefully attentive in the difficult driving conditions.

Suddenly, I found myself driving on the shoulder, and my heart started pounding because I knew I had not driven myself onto that shoulder. Time seemed to stand still as I saw that the car in front of me had suddenly turned off the highway and onto a side road. My mind raced as I fought back fear and confusion. Then I saw a semitractor-trailer coming toward me—I thought he was going to take off my side mirror as we met. There he was, in my lane, with his lane full of cars. Had I not been supernaturally taken off the highway, I would have been hit head-on by that semi. Only God could have done this for me: removing my car and me from certain destruction.

Meanwhile, my husband was also on that same highway, coming from the opposite direction. He saw the semi in front of him, switching back and forth from lane to lane. When he reached for his phone to call me, he was led to not call. He said it seemed as though the Lord pushed his hand away from his cell phone. So he settled back and began praying for me.

Still moving forward, I drove back onto the highway and headed for my destination. Needless to say, I was significantly moved by the event, knowing I had just experienced a divine rescue. I must admit that I am still a bit shaken, often finding myself crying tears of joy and wonder. I am incredibly grateful to inform you that this week I was not hit head-on by a semi. I continue to live and to tell you about the goodness of God and His faithful commitment to His covenant promise found in Psalm 91.

KIM HULL

Our children attend a wonderful Christian school, and they have chapel every Monday morning with guest speakers coming to speak to the students about different topics to encourage them in their walk with Christ. One such Monday morning, my son was singing and helping to lead worship prior to the speaker coming forward to share. I came to the chapel time to watch the praise team sing and was able to hear Angelia Schum speak to the students. We had never met, but I knew her by sight. After she spoke and during the quiet time, she turned around and asked my name. I affirmed that I was who she was inquiring about, and she started telling me about a dream she had in which my children and I were in a car wreck, and in the dream I was killed. She was very kind about it and didn't alarm me, but she explained that she believed sometimes dreams were prophetic and she felt she needed to share the dream with me. After we talked awhile, she prayed some of the scripture of Psalm 91 for me and also prayed that any assignment of Satan be broken over me and my family. I thanked her, and, at peace, I left and continued on with my busy life.

The next fall, the Sunday before school was to start, I had dropped a friend's daughter off after our evening church service. I came to a stoplight near her home and stopped, and then as the light turned green I proceeded through the intersection. A drunk driver going sixty-five miles an hour down one of the main streets in our small town hit the front corner of the passenger side of our car. My car was completely spun around in the middle of the intersection on two tires before it came to rest and started smoking. I quickly urged all the children to get out of the car and head to the grass on the side of the road. My car was demolished, and the air bag on the driver's side of the other car deployed. One of the young men in our car slammed his elbow on the window, and it was sore, but other than that we walked away from a wreck that should have been devastating. We later discovered the friend who had bumped his elbow had a small fracture, which had to be casted, but that was the only injury. I believe with all my heart that if Angie had not shared her dream and prayed for our family, that wreck's outcome would have been totally different. I praise God for His provision and promise in Psalm 91 that He will take care of us.

HUDSON BAY PLANE CRASH

My youngest son, Andrew, had recently returned from his second tour of duty in Afghanistan. This last one had been one of those long, fifteen-month tours. He had served twelve months in Afghanistan earlier, with a year break in between. I spent many hours praying protection over him. Psalm 91 became particularly meaningful to me, and I would pray this protection psalm over him on a daily basis. I would pray: "God will deliver him from the snare of the fowler," and "He will give His angels charge over him to guard him in all his ways." It was such a relief this time when he returned, because his active duty commitment to the army was up and he was returning to civilian life.

Andrew wanted to celebrate his return with a trip to New York for his fiancée's birthday. We were to pick him up at the airport the evening of January 15. It had been a sweet, sweet time for Stephanie and him, and his dad and I were looking forward to his coming home and spending time with us.

The phone rang, and it was Andrew calling. He started the conversation with, "I'm all right." My husband's immediate thought was, "Well, of course you are." Then Andrew proceeded to tell his dad that his plane just went down in the Hudson River and to turn on the TV. That was all he had time to tell us. His dad and I rushed to turn on the TV. There was breaking news of Flight 1549 crashing into the Hudson River. We stared incredulously at the screen as we saw the footage of this airplane just floating in the water. The right wing was listing. We watched and waited to hear from him again.

When he called again, he told us he and Stephanie had been on the right wing of the plane, which had been sinking. They had stepped out in frigid water up to their ankles, and it wasn't long before the water was rising up above their knees. They were being pushed farther and farther to the tip of the wing as more passengers came out of the emergency door.

As Andrew recalled the events of the day, he said he knew there was something wrong with the airplane when he heard a loud pop and then saw black smoke coming from the engine. As the plane banked to make a turn, Andrew reassured Stephanie that it would be all right; they weren't far out from the airport, and the plane was returning to land. As they looked out the window, Andrew realized there was a strange silence on the airplane. Usually you can hear the hum of the engines, but he couldn't hear any engine at all. At that time he knew they were only gliding. Losing altitude quickly, he knew they were in trouble. When the pilot came over the intercom and told them to brace for impact, Stephanie was crying, and Andrew knew they would be going down in the water. He said he was somewhat relieved that they would be going into the water rather than hitting land. He thought that might give them more of a chance for survival. He said he had a spark of hope, mingled with fear. He was telling Stephanie that if they somehow survived the crash, that they would need to get off of the plane in a hurry. They kissed each other, said "I love you," huddled close to one another, and started praying together, bracing for the impact.

Andrew said he had all kinds of scenarios running through his head in that one long minute they had before the impact. What if the plane tears apart and they get sucked down into the water? He would possibly be frantically trying to find Stephanie. He also knew hypothermia could take over quickly, and their lungs could freeze rapidly, along with their extremities. He thought, "I made it through two deployments to Afghanistan, and now it's going to end like this?"

By the grace of God and with the experience of a very skilled pilot, the airplane did a relatively smooth landing on the water. They unbuckled their seat belts quickly, and Andrew guided Stephanie down the aisle to the emergency door on the wing.

Andrew comforts Stephanie after the crash.

The pilot, Captain Sullenberger, was at the terminal where Andrew was taken. He seemed calm, drinking a cup of coffee, with one of his hands in his pocket. I'm sure, though, that he also was in a state of shock. There was much celebration and thanks being given to him from everyone at the terminal. God had certainly used him that day.

Once Andrew and Stephanie arrived at our home by train, we all praised God and marveled at the miracle that had taken place. We rejoiced at the witness by Andrew of how God was all over that flight—placing Chesley Sullenberger at the helm of the plane that day; the often-busy Hudson waterway being clear of ferries, barges, and boats; keeping the plane in one piece and afloat while all 155 passengers were rescued; firmly planting their almost frozen feet on a slippery surface, in a swift current, and not allowing them to fall. Witnessing and experiencing this miracle firsthand has strengthened and affirmed Andrew's faith.

Could it be that all those prayers, particularly the protection prayer of Psalm 91 that I prayed over Andrew while he was deployed, continued to cover my son? Absolutely! He had survived two long tours of duty in Afghanistan, and now upon his return, he is a survivor again. I believe the covering of his dad and my prayers over our son helped carry him to safety that day. God's dramatic display of His protection was evident. My own personal thought is that Captain Sullenberger was really just the co-pilot that day. The real pilot, God Himself, was in control of that flight!

Our faithfulness in claiming God's Word and praying those words back to Him carries over into our daily lives, whether we are praying them for daily comfort, strength, and protection or praying them through a difficult time. God was with my youngest son in Afghanistan, and He was with him on that airplane. No matter what the circumstances:

> He who dwells in the shelter of the Most High
> Will abide in the shadow of the Almighty.
> I will say to the LORD, "My refuge and my fortress,
> My God, in whom I trust!"
>
> —PSALM 91:1–2

Andrew with his parents in their home

There has been more good news that followed since that day. You might enjoy knowing that the First Officer Jeff Skiles and his wife came to Andrew and Stephanie's wedding and reception on August 22. They were delightful, and it gave them all a chance to hug him and thank him for helping to make the day possible!

Andrew and Stephanie celebrating life

Captain Sullenberger and his wife regretted not being able to attend, so they sent a personal video to play at the wedding, congratulating Andrew and Stephanie on their special day and giving them a tip or two about how to have a happy marriage! It was so neat.

FRED AND BOBBIE STRICKLAND

In every life there are days of joy and days of tragedy, days of peace and days when everything you've ever believed about God's faithfulness is put to the test. An early day in May 2000 was such a day in our lives.

Early that morning we sat together and prayed, as we usually do before a trip. We prayed God's protection over us that we would arrive safely to San Angelo, Texas, where we were scheduled to pick up a large U-Haul moving truck, unload all our furniture from storage, and move it all to Glen Rose, Texas, our new home. We had been staying in Glen Rose for a few days at our son's house while looking for a rental house. We had found one, and this was moving day. Fred had just retired a few weeks before from a small school west of San Angelo. After being principal there for four years and finally retiring, he was elated at the prospect of his retirement days of enjoyment! But what should have been a day of great happiness turned into a day of trauma and pain.

Rain had been pelting Highway 67 from Glen Rose to Stephenville since early morning. Dark clouds hovered over the entire area, and we were aware that we should travel safely, for the highway was slick. We had approached a truck and trailer going very slowly. To get around the truck, Fred had to accelerate, and when he did, he began to hydroplane. "Bobbie Kaye, we're going off the road," he said. "I'm losing control! I'm losing control!" And in that freeze-framed moment, in what seemed like slow motion, our fully loaded truck began to turn over repeatedly, several times, until finally the motion subsided, and we sat upright in a farmer's field.

Through years of teaching from the Bible, we had come to know that words are literally a matter of life or death. My words from Psalm 91 that day as our truck was flipping over and over literally erupted up out of my spirit and through my mouth: "Father, because we have loved You, therefore You will deliver us! You will set us securely on high because we have known Your name! You *have given your angels charge over us to keep us in all our ways! Thank You, Father, for saving us!*" Because the truck had landed right side up, I quickly breathed a prayer of thanks and looked over at my husband. He was deathly pale with blood trickling down both sides of his head. I knew in that moment that he was critically injured, but again the spirit and the Word of God rose up in me, and I shouted at him, "You will live and not die, and declare the works of the Lord!"

Then, after grabbing Fred's briefcase, I quickly exited the smoking vehicle and walked up toward the highway for help. A young woman who had been behind us on the highway saw us go off the road, and had already called 911. We knew later that God had strategically placed just the right person behind us that day, so that someone could be there to help us. It turned out that she had been a former student of Fred during the days when he had been a vice principal at Glen Rose High School, years before. She knew us! She then quickly made me sit down on the ground, telling me that I looked to be in shock, all the while assuring me that help was on the way.

In the meantime, Fred sat alone in a smoking truck, not knowing if he would live or die. He began to talk to the Lord, repenting and asking for help. He was aware that no one was there helping him and wondered why he'd been left there alone. As fearful thoughts began to envelop him, he suddenly felt a firm warm hand on his shoulder and heard the sweet gentle words of a woman saying to him, "Honey, you're going to be all right. Everything is going to be all right." Days later, as he remembered this terrifying moment in the truck, he would tell me and others about the woman coming to him. He asked us who it was. I told him that no one went back to that truck until the paramedics came—not I or our former student. There had been no one out in that field but him. But *someone* had spoken to him and reassured him. *Someone had definitely been there!* Who could be there with him? An angel? Yes, I believe an angel came that day to help my husband.

Fred was eventually removed from the crushed truck by the paramedics, who came sometime later. We went to the Stephenville hospital, were checked out, and I was found to be in fairly good shape. Fred, however, was sent to the trauma unit at Harris Hospital in Ft. Worth. His head had been severely injured by a computer and steel toolbox that had been in the backseat of the truck. Apparently, they both hit his head as the truck rolled. His scalp was practically all removed from his head, and his back had been broken in several places. His entire body had been traumatized from all the contents of the backseat of the truck falling on him. He knew he was seriously injured. But God was faithful.

The doctors told Fred that the MRIs had indicated that several vertebrae had been broken and that his head was injured to the point that he surely would endure permanent brain damage. They built Fred a body cast to be worn every day, which was made of a hard acrylic. It looked like a Roman soldier's shield and went from neck to hip. He was told that he should have to wear it for six months to a year, maybe longer. He would become addicted to the painkillers and would face that also. Their prognosis was one of hopelessness and despair. But God was faithful. He had also said in Psalm 91 that He would satisfy us with a long life (v. 16). We knew that Fred could have that life if he would only *believe* and *trust*. We believed, we trusted, and God was faithful.

In two or three months, Fred was able to remove the cast, and his head was healed from the critical brain injury that he was supposed to have. By autumn he was coaching in a Christian school! Praise His holy name!

Many, many times in our lives we have been assaulted by the devil and by life itself. We've had many chances to despair, but we have learned that we can always stand on His holy Word. Psalm 91 is our covenant, and God is faithful if we believe and confess it. It is forever settled in heaven. God is good, and His mercy endures forever.

CAPTAIN DEL HICKS: PLANE CRASH INTO THE ATLANTIC OCEAN

Sometimes when you find out about Psalm 91, it is for a special purpose. God knew that Psalm 91 would mean the difference between life and death for Pat and Del Hicks.

Pat had bought a large Bible with everything God has spoken in red at a gospel quartet concert. Many Bibles have the words of Jesus printed in red, but she had never seen one that had *red* in the Old Testament as well. While looking through her new Bible, she noticed that Psalm 91 had verses 14, 15, and 16 in red. The psalmist was speaking in the first part of the chapter, and then God answered him back! Pat stared at the words in red. Then she immediately took her new Bible to show her pastor what she had found. "Have you seen this before?" she asked. He was so impressed with what she showed him that he preached from this psalm for the next six weeks. And it certainly paid off. The day came that Pat and Del, along with their church family, needed what they had learned in Psalm 91 to pray in faith for Del's life!

Del Hicks was a boat captain who often sailed along the Florida coast, but today he was flying home from Chub Cay, Bahamas. He expected to be home much sooner than his normal mode of travel. However, this was not a pleasure flight, but a flight home for a friend's funeral. At age fifty-eight, he had lost two close friends within a few months of each other.

Suddenly, thirty-five minutes into the 125-mile flight, the engines of the Piper Seneca didn't sound right. Del leaned up to take a look at the radar screen in front of the pilot. They were about 50 miles east of Ft. Lauderdale and 25 miles from the island of Bimini when the twin-engine plane lost one engine. The pilot reacted by ordering luggage to be thrown out the exit door. When the second engine stopped, the tiny aircraft fell to the ocean. The pilot had taken classes on emergency landings and remembered to put the tail down first and skid over the water. It floated just long enough for them to get out of the plane, slide down the wings, and into the waters of the Atlantic. They had about five minutes before it sank. The sudden crash prevented the pilot from sending a distress signal. And three hours later, the group realized the plane's ELT (emergency locator transmitter) did not fire either.

Everyone (the four passengers and the pilot) was now bobbing in the salty, cold waters of the Atlantic. Del was the first out since he was closest to the door; then an attorney and his wife who had chartered the plane; their large cocker spaniel, Chaco; Dan Tuckfield; and last, the pilot. (Chaco had traveled with them all over the world, but interestingly, this trip he did not want to go. It was as though he sensed some impending danger. To get Chaco in the car and later in the plane, he had to be picked up and carried. That was highly unusual. He generally loved to travel.) When they hit the water, they discovered a whole new set of problems. The attorney's wife did not know how to swim, the dog went berserk, and as soon as they were in the water, all of their teeth went into a rhythmic chatter. It was about 55 degrees that day when they entered the water. (Later when a news reporter in a wet suit was being filmed on location to demonstrate their ordeal, his body could not tolerate the cold. He was forced to get out.)

Most of the group wanted to swim toward Bimini, but Del knew the strong current would sweep them away, so they gave up that idea. Del's knowledge of the tides and currents was invaluable to keep them from being swept away from the land that was twenty miles away. Dan

Tuckfield was an expert swimmer and succeeded in diving twenty feet down to where the plane was resting on the bottom of the ocean and was able to bring up a ten-foot canvas tarp, life vests, and his wet suit. God was certainly with them, because this was the first time he had taken his swimming gear onto an airplane with him, and that gear turned out to be invaluable. Dan attached a line to each end of the tarp and then dove down and tied it to the tail of the plane. Then each person tied himself to the other end of the line, and the airplane held them secure against the tide. For four hours this kept them from being pulled into the Gulf Stream or crashing on the rocks. When no rescue planes came, they knew the emergency signal had not worked, so they decided to start swimming toward the light.

Since the only lady on the plane couldn't swim, she was totally dependent on being held up by Del or Dan. Finally, Del supported her head, holding her up under her armpits, and Dan held her legs over his shoulders while fighting the choppy waves with an exhausted dog that was trying to stay balanced on her floating torso. Her weight, along with the cold water and the two-foot waves that kept pounding against the swimmers, made it an almost impossible battle. So after two hours, they decided to tie themselves together and just tread water since they hadn't made any distance by attempting to swim.

Del and his wife, Pat, had been quoting the promises from Psalm 91 every day for months. For the first time he now realized what God had been preparing him for, so he began quoting those familiar verses. Del was wondering what was going on with his wife, Pat, right now. By now she would know that they were in trouble, and she would be praying. He knew that, and he was right. The Coast Guard's biggest search in Florida's history had already begun. Pat was doing her part when she realized he was in trouble. She stood at the private airport watching the sky. She too was reminding God of Del's faith and dependence on Him. At one point she put her face in the wall of the customs room where she was standing and came to the realization his plane was not coming in. She buried her face and poured out her heart to God. She said, "I may not know where Del is right now, but I know where he lives! He lives in the refuge of the Most High. Wherever he is right now, you are his God." And Pat was not the only one praying. Pastors, friends, family, and church members were continually lifting Del up and reminding God of His promises. Pat knew they had a covenant with Almighty God, so she continued to pray in the Spirit and confess God's promises until morning.

All night through the nightmare ordeal of being lost at sea, Del held the attorney's wife's legs until his own leg cramps made it impossible for him to use the lower part of his body. It was all they could do to keep her head above the water. Her husband, the attorney, had come up with a plan where he stayed awake all night, calling out the names of everyone in the group to make sure they were all right. By daybreak he was desperate. Having swallowed too much salt water in the rough seas, panicked, he finally gave up, took away all precautions, and let himself slip to his death before anyone had a chance to reason with him. The men attempted to revive him, but it was too late. They now had a non-swimmer clinging to a dog and also the body of her husband to manage. Del's body was severely bruised from the battering of the waves and the attempt to keep everyone afloat. The group fiercely held on to the body in hopes of giving him a Christian burial, but that afternoon the smell of death brought up a ten-foot tiger shark, one of the most dangerous sharks in the ocean. The shark was nose to nose with Del, and his survival went from virtually impossible to a whole new meaning. He had always had a healthy fear of sharks, but as he was looking that shark in the eye, it surprised him that the promises in Psalm 91 had so filled his heart that he didn't feel any fear. He knew he was protected. They were finally, however, forced to let go of the body, and the shark disappeared.

As hours passed, Del couldn't remember ever being so tired and cold. They were twenty miles from land. It had been an emotional nightmare, as well as the biggest physical test of his life. But then, the sound of a helicopter engine brought Del instantly alert. They waved their arms to get the pilot's attention, but he passed by. That, on top of losing her husband, must have been too much for this poor, brokenhearted woman who was being kept from drowning by two of the stronger swimmers, because late that afternoon, she gave up and died. Del decided to take his faith to the next level and do exactly as the Scriptures commanded. He began to just speak forth praises to his God. With every hour, that is all he set his mind on—to speak His praise out loud.

Pat thought of their thirty-eight years of marriage. Not even daring to try to sleep, she fought with the devil as he hit her mind with vain imaginations. The enemy would remind her of the two friends who died, an utterance would tell her she would never hear Del's voice again, and as she closed her eyes, she would see the plane crash, the fire, the water. The voice would mock her (naming the friends who recently died), telling her, "Bob died in June! Gene died a few days ago! What makes you think Del isn't dead? Everyone knows death comes in threes!"

"No!" Pat resisted. "I have a covenant. I will not fear! I will not be afraid of the terror by night!" And she would resist that type of terror that especially comes at night. As morning came, she had never slept. The morning gave Pat hope. Surely, with all the searchers, they would find Del; there was comfort in something being done. There were three Coast Guard stations, sixteen private planes, and numerous other boats involved in what was the largest search-and-rescue effort in Florida, but the day dragged on with no success. That many looking, and still no sign! What was a mind to do with that information? Pat said that she just continued to listen to a teaching tape on Psalm 91, turning it over and playing it time and again to keep her faith strong.

Neighbors would come over and try to *help* Pat *face the facts*. She would gracefully slip them back out the door and tell them, "I'll get back with you when I have some fresh news!" Pat clung to her faith. Wondering if she was hanging on to just hope, she needed a word from the Lord. She went to her daily scripture box and pulled out the card for that day—*think on things that are pure, that are good*! That was enough for her. God was telling her to think on a good report and let her mind dwell on that.

In tragic situations, reporters try to find out how the loved ones are coping. They are looking for a piece of information from the family to broadcast on the news to the outside world. When reporters asked Pat how she was managing to stay so calm, she explained that it was the peace of God. That was Pat's answer to the world.

Del had never been so cold in his entire life. He said that, try as he would, he could not remember what it felt like to be warm. The three remaining passengers decided to swim for land. Dan Tuckfield knew they would all die unless he could make it to the island, so Dan told the pilot to keep an eye on Del and took off. However, it didn't take long for the pilot and Del to become separated in the waves. Del drifted into unconsciousness, and Chaco, the dog he had been holding, was lost into the sea.

Dan's experience as competitive swimmer helped him as he made his way for the shores of the Bahamas. Thank God for his wet suit and fins. The miracle is that this was the first time in all of his flying this route that he had brought his dive equipment. God certainly provides what we need. Dan Tuckfield needed to get to shore.

Something supernatural happened on Thursday, the second morning of the ordeal. Through this night a member of the Hicks' church had stayed up praying specifically for one thing—that sharks would not attack Del. She prayed into the early hours of the morning before she rested. At six o'clock that morning, Pat Hicks had awakened with joy bursting out of her heart. Pat recalled, "I came straight up out of my bed. A peace flooded me like I'd never felt. Del is going to be all right." Through the night there had still been no news given to her from any of the rescuers—they had not located the plane, not one passenger had been located dead or alive, there was no evidence whatsoever that anything had changed, yet Pat woke everyone in the house saying, "Let's worship God. It's over." She dressed and waited for the call. By faith she put on Del's favorite perfume. When she called the parsonage, the pastor's wife told her husband, "We must get to Pat. She's lost it." But Pat's supernatural joy was contagious, and the whole group had a worship service.

Finally, at eight o'clock they called the Coast Guard, and the guy said, "I'm sorry. I can't talk right now. We have just found someone, and the helicopter is lifting off the pad." They had spotted a floating yellow life vest, and it looked like it had a corpse in it. There was an unconscious, frozen Del Hicks drifting in the ocean.

Dan had swum throughout the night, and it wasn't until the next morning at dawn that he had finally stumbled to the shore. After notifying the Coast Guard of the two survivors' location, it was nine o'clock when they spotted what they thought was a corpse, but, thank God, it was not a corpse. Del was unconscious—but he was alive. When Del was first seen below, he was not moving and looked to be dead. It is the policy to leave the dead victims and pick up all survivors first, but the helicopter pilot prayed, "Lord, if he is alive, let him move something." Even thought Del was unconscious, it was at that moment that he lifted his arm. Instantly, they came in to make the pick up. When rescue workers could not bend his frozen legs to put him in a basket, they finally laid him across it and used it as a lift.

Del Hicks standing with two Coast Guard officers
who helped rescue him from the Atlantic

It was obvious that God's angels were watching over him, because there were no sharks in sight of his unconscious body. However, an hour later when the pilot was found and rescued alive, he had a different story—he had been swimming for his life because he was surrounded by sharks at the moment of his rescue. They were circling closer and closer, getting ready to move in for the kill. The pilot had actually named the ten-foot sharks as the circle got smaller and smaller. Miraculously, even though Del was unconscious, God had kept the sharks away from him as surely as Daniel in the lions' den had been protected from the lions. When Dan was told that Del had been rescued alive, tears ran down his face. He said, "I knew he would make it! He had the faith."

Del was admitted to Jackson Memorial Hospital with a body temperature of only 83 degrees. He was placed on a machine to keep his heart and lungs going while they circulated his blood through a warmer. All day and night Pat stood over his bed waiting for him to wake up, but finally, the God of the Ninety-first Psalm kept His promise, and Del awoke to rejoice and give God the glory.

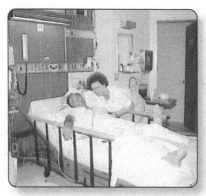

Del and Pat in his room at Jackson Memorial Hospital

During the week that Del was in the hospital, he and Pat prayed for practically everyone on staff. Once, the entire staff of student nurses was brought in for Del and Pat to pray over each person's life. After making sure that they were all born again, they prayed over them that they would begin to pray over others. That week had even a greater testimony as people came out of the woodwork for prayer. They prayed with nurses and patients—from the intensive care unit to the waiting room.

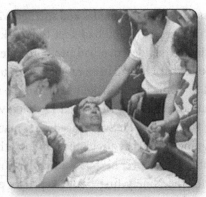

Many came to Del's room to pray for his healing.

The week had been truly blessed by God, but the battle wasn't over. A couple of years after Del left the hospital, a two-foot-long blood clot

A banner welcomes Del back home after his stay in the hospital and gives God the glory for his recovery.

formed in his leg as a result of the blood recirculation procedure. His leg was swollen to double its normal size, and the clot was inoperable. Although Del had survived the ocean, the doctors told Del and Pat that the clot could progress through his system and kill him at any time. Again, the Hicks prayed. A few weeks later on the way back from the Bahamas, the situation became critical. However, the salvation of Del from the ocean wasn't the Lord's only miracle— the tests confirmed the blood clot was gone!

DEL AND PAT HICKS: SAVED FROM HURRICANE ANDREW

Pat and Del Hicks, seasoned from living in Florida, were both familiar with storms and hurricanes and knew it was important to *live* prepared. They had survived four hurricanes and were now facing Andrew. Their windows and doors were covered over with plywood, water had been stored in the barrels they kept handy, and they had even filled their bathtubs with water. Everything outside that was not securely held down was brought inside, and extra food was on their shelves. Pat listened to the latest weather report and realized the storm was headed straight for Miami, with winds exceeding 150 miles per hour, putting their home directly in its path. Del walked in about that time, telling everyone that there were cars bumper to bumper along every lane of highway leaving the city, moving no more than 5 miles per hour, thus extinguishing all hope that they could load up the family and get out of town.

It had just been a year before that Del had been in an airplane crash that left him in the cold waters of the Atlantic for three days as he held tight to Psalm 91 until he was rescued. He had survived the airplane crash, the sharks that circled the survivors, and the turbulent icy waters of the ocean by day and by night. With all of that experience, he was more determined than ever that the enemy would not get victory over his family this time.

Pat looked at the palms and favorite maple trees in her yard that had provided shade and fun for their children and grandchildren for the last two generations, and she too was determined that the enemy would not be able to win. A hurricane wind of 150 miles per hour was nothing to sneeze at, but Pat knew she had authority in the name of Jesus over anything the enemy might send. She began to encourage herself by remembering how Moses had applied the lamb's blood to the doorposts of his house when the death angel devastated Egypt, so she began to apply the blood of Jesus Christ and quote the promises of Psalm 91. She felt like she was always coming to the Lord with the Ninety-first Psalm. "I know there are other Scripture promises I could stand on, but I've got this psalm down in my heart, and I know it's as true today as the day it was first spoken; therefore, I will continue to declare, 'We dwell in the secret place of the Most High.' We say into the heavenlies that you are our God and our refuge in this storm!" Pat walked through the yard laying hands on the trees, confessing that they were now under the shadow of the Almighty, and then touching the house, the utility shed, and placing everything under the protection of the God of the universe.

Fourteen family members gathered in the Hicks' home to wait out the storm. Outside the rain raged, and by 2:00 a.m. there was no electrical power. To add to the problem, Pat was having to carefully limit her mother's oxygen for the supply to last. As the storm strengthened, they could hear things crashing into the house. In fact, all through the long hours of the night, they could hear heavy objects beating against their home. By 4:00 a.m. the storm was so vicious everyone thought the house would break in two. It sounded like a jet taking off the runway. When it became obvious that they were going to lose the roof, they all began to lay hands on the walls and command them to stand strong in the name of Jesus. The roof convulsed, but it continued to hold its position. That was such a testimony to everyone that the name of Jesus was greater and had more power than any hurricane. Del had purchased a battery-operated television, so all fourteen people piled up on their king-sized bed and watched the storm. On the radar, they were able to watch the eyewall moving inland. Their house was in a direct line parallel to the weather service's hurricane center, and they were able to see the high winds hit the hurricane center and take out their wind meter, their radar, and clear the top of the building. The last reading on the meter before it blew off the hurricane center showed winds of 163 miles per hour. Then the TV coverage went out. By this time there was a continuous barrage of things being smashed against the house. Pat said, "It sounded like a freight train, the noise was so loud. At the time we thought it was cars hitting the house." It was too dark to see clearly out the window, but they were able to see that items were flying past. At one point something crashed so loudly in the backyard that they decided their shed must have blown apart. It was not until 7:00 a.m. that the storm began to subside. When they were finally able to go outside, it looked like pictures from a movie of a city that had been bombed. Del said, "Sheds were hanging from electrical wires, half the house directly behind us was missing, most of the roofs in the neighborhood were gone or damaged extensively, debris was strewn everywhere, and trees were uprooted. All kinds of things were draped over the wires that were left standing. Someone's canoe was even hanging by the wires. Our home was the only one in the area with a shed intact. The doors to the shed were blown open, but everything was still inside." Pat checked her maple tree in the backyard. The tree was stood back up, replanted, and continued to grow beautifully.

Pat said, "Our property looked like an oasis in a desert, and soon it became like a tourist attraction." Neighbors were appalled when they saw the damage in the neighborhood compared to the Hicks' property. One man wanted to know what on earth they had done to protect their place. He was suspicious: "You've been praying again, haven't you?" Pat explained that she had walked around the corners of her property praying Psalm 91. Seeing that the Hicks still had every tree, their roof was not gone, and their shed was still in place, he asked her to extend her prayer borders! Pat told the man she would have if she had had more time, but she had been busy trying to get her mom situated.

Hurricane Andrew's fury left the Hicks' shed untouched.

The Hicks' protection extended to others, as well. For the next three weeks, family members and friends whose homes were destroyed came to live with the Hicks. There were fourteen people living in their four-bedroom, two-bathroom home, without electricity. When people were finally allowed to drive through the area, Pat said that she could not keep from crying as they traveled through the forty-mile disaster. All she could say was, "The devastation was beyond description, and it broke my heart to see how many people had lost property and possessions at the hand of the enemy."

When the insurance adjuster came and saw their three big, beautiful trees healthily standing in the front yard, he was flabbergasted, since at least 75 percent of the plant life had been destroyed in their area.

It was not until he got inside and saw Pat proofreading her magazine article of God's goodness and protection that he said, "I knew it! I knew it!" Pat had him come over and read the article. He looked like he was glad to finally have an answer for their property withstanding the hurricane. He said, "I knew there had to be something more to it. God must have been the one protecting for you to have gone through this storm practically untouched."

Hurricane Andrew was a category five storm. Sixty-five people lost their lives, more than 250,000 were left homeless, and 82,000 businesses were destroyed. One hundred thousand people left Dade County, deciding not to live there anymore. It caused $26.5 billion of damage, which is the equivalent of $41.3 billion and thirty-three years worth of debris. I can imagine that as the insurance adjuster made a list of the claim, he knew that insurance companies wished that more people knew to pray Psalm 91!

Del and Pat continue to thank God for the name of Jesus. They both say that they are determined more than ever to start each day with the Ninety-first Psalm. In fact, their exact statement was, "Psalm 91 is, and always will be, our refuge in every storm."

Del and Pat Hicks

MRS. MARY (DON) JOHNSON: KIDNAPPING TESTIMONY

Author's Note: Mary tells in her own words the testimony of her kidnapping miracle. It is a dramatic account of the power of God's deliverance and protection.

After just returning from a five-day Red Brangus cow sale where my husband and I also met our daughter to buy clothes for our soon-to-be-birthed first grandchild, I had gotten an early start that morning to catch up on my chores. We live twelve miles out in the country, so I was surprised to be interrupted by a young man in an old van—supposedly lost—asking for a drink of water. The pretense was over when he pulled a gun and told me to get in the car. My surprised scream was soon stifled when he threatened my life if I did that again. I was thrown into the back of the van where a man wearing a nylon stocking on his head put athletic tape over my mouth and hands and covered my head with a black windbreaker. Black shag carpet covered the sides, floor, and roof of the van. The windows were covered with black curtains.

I couldn't tell where they were taking me. I know we crossed railroad tracks and ended up on a gravel road. I had never been so frightened in my life. All I could think about was that I was soon to be fifty—soon to be a grandmother—and I wasn't sure I would live to see either. But my greatest fear was being raped. Finally, however, I came to my senses and started claiming my spiritual covenant promise of protection. I suddenly realized that *I was a child of God—fear was of the devil—and I had the protection of God on my life.*

By this time we had stopped. With a wool cap pulled down over my face, I was led over a barbed-wire fence and across a pasture to an old, abandoned ranch house where I was handcuffed to the bathroom lavatory pipes. One of my kidnappers asked, "What would be the best way to get your husband to cooperate without alerting the police?" Then I was warned if he went to the police he would never see me again—alive! A phone call with all the usual kidnapping threats and instructions was planned, and then I was left to my dilemma.

Still quoting my promises, singing hymns of deliverance, and thanking God, I was frantically working to get the pipes loose, but they wouldn't budge. God said in Psalm 91:15, "In your day of trouble, call upon Me, and I will answer." I started praying, "Lord, I am calling on You! I can't do this, but You can. Show me a way to get loose." Then for the first time I noticed a tiny pipe coming up the back of the sink. I don't have any idea how I was able to break through, but I know it was a miracle because the FBI agent couldn't believe I was able to do what I did.

Feeling sure the kidnappers would make their call to Don and be back shortly, I was out the back door and over the fence in no time. I had no idea where I was, but I was confident that God would get me where I needed to be. Twelve miles later I came to a house with every door locked except the front door. (I later found out the owner never left her doors unlocked, except on this particular day.) After several calls, the sheriff was on his way to get me, but my husband had already left for Goldthwaite, Texas, with the ransom money.

The kidnappers skipped the first meeting, but called at twelve thirty that night with a new appointed place to meet in Austin, Texas. Obviously they didn't know I had escaped. This time it was the Texas Rangers who met and took the first man into custody; later, the second one was apprehended. I was called to Austin by the FBI to pick him out of a *lineup*. All I asked was for the men in the lineup to wear a ball cap and say, "Would you get me a glass of water?" With that, I was able to successfully pick him out of the group, and my job was over.

I thank God for His covenant of protection in Psalm 91. We do not have to be afraid of the "terror of what man can do to us—it will not approach us."

Author's Note: The man who was convicted of this crime was no amateur criminal. According to police, he had a habitual crime problem since his youth and had previously been convicted and imprisoned for robbery, indecency, and sexual assault. For this present offense he was sentenced to ninety-nine years in prison. The sheriff told Mary Johnson they had never had anyone in their local jail as malicious as this man. The FBI was shocked Mary was able to escape and even more shocked that she had not been beaten, raped, or murdered. One of the FBI agents made the comment, "We cannot believe we are sitting here today with you, and you are alive and well."

Few people understand the power of this wonderful covenant.

JULIE'S MIRACLE

as told by her father

Julie's ordeal began in May 1983, while she attended a friend's birthday party in the country. Julie had ridden horses with her grandfather for nearly nine of her ten years, so when they asked who wanted to ride, she jumped at the chance. But a ten-year-old riding bareback on a grown horse has very little to hold on to—so when the horse began to run, she slipped under its belly. And between the rocks and the hooves she received a very serious head injury.

When we arrived at the hospital, a physician friend tried to be a buffer for us before we saw our daughter. He warned us that she was in very serious condition and that the hospital was already making arrangements to have her transported to the nearest large city for treatment. Even with his attempt to prepare us, we were still not anywhere close to being prepared for what we saw. The right side of her head was swollen literally to the size of a volleyball. Both eyes were swollen shut, and her hair and face were drenched in blood. There was no way we could have recognized her.

I need, at this point, to interject some crucial information. Through the teachings of Kenneth Copeland of Kenneth Copeland Ministries in Fort Worth, I had started doing a great deal of study on healing and faith. Jesus and I had spent a lot of time alone together, during which I received the baptism of the Holy Spirit, and the Lord became very personal to me. Our church was strong on believing that Jesus is still the *healer*. I can truly say that from the instant I first saw Julie's condition, I called on Jesus and totally expected that His healing power and His promises in Psalm 91 would bring her through. I'm glad I didn't have to analyze the situation, but we all knew it was so bad that we had to have a miracle. Even before the ambulance reached the hospital, there was a growing network of believers who were interceding.

In addition to the driver, there were two paramedics in the back of the ambulance with Julie, and one in the front between the driver and me. I prayed all the way—just in a whisper—almost oblivious to the others in the cab. I remember thanking Jesus for her healing and telling Satan that he couldn't have Julie—that she was a child of God and had been dedicated to the Lord from birth. For the entire eighty-five miles I never stopped claiming her healing. I didn't get loud! I knew I was being heard in both realms of the spirit. Then somewhere just this side of Abilene, the paramedics slid the panel open between the back and the cab area and said something to the driver. We had been going fairly fast all the way, but at this point the driver put on his siren and sped the rest of the way to the hospital. I found out later that the paramedics had informed the driver that Julie had lost all vital signs and could not be revived. I'm not sure how long she had no vital signs, but it was more than a few minutes. I learned that life came back into her body about the time we came to the edge of town.

While all this was happening, my brother-in-law, who was an elder in our church, was about forty-five minutes behind us in his car. On the way he felt that God told him Julie had died, and God asked him if he would be willing to lie across her body like the prophet Elisha had done with the little boy in 2 Kings 4:34 to bring him back to life. Realizing this meant he would most likely have to push his way past the doctors and nurses and look very foolish, he said that he wrestled within himself for several minutes before knowing without a doubt that he was willing to do it. The moment the commitment was made, he felt God told him Julie would be all right. We later backtracked to the place where he was en route during this confrontation with God. According to our calculations, the ambulance would have been coming into the city limits just about the time God told him that Julie would be all right. That was when her vital signs had returned.

Upon our arrival Julie was immediately taken in for a CAT scan. When the doctor got the results, her skull was cracked like an eggshell with so many complications that he gave us no hope whatsoever. Someone asked him if there would be brain damage, and he replied, "Parents always want to ask about brain damage. Your concern needs to be whether or not she will live through the night, but if she does live, yes, there will be extensive brain damage." I was not arrogant, but I denied each negative statement from anyone who was not standing in faith with us. The doctor was obviously perturbed with us, but I'm sure he just thought we were in denial. He just didn't realize where our denial was coming from. To the doctor's total surprise, Julie did live through the night. We kept healing scriptures on her pillow at all times and held her and spoke love to her continuously. My wife had the astronomical job of cleaning the dried blood from her hair and untangling it—speaking healing and quoting Psalm 91 over her the whole time.

We were informed we were in for a long stay, but my frustration was that Julie wasn't climbing out of the bed the next day, ready to go home. God must have given me a *gift of faith* because I was ready for a Lazarus healing. We began to notice that, miraculously, nearly every timetable we were given was accomplished seven times faster. At first we thought it was a neat coincidence, until it continued way beyond any possibility of happenstance.

During the hospital stay of only nine days, we saw our miracle unveil. The physical damage continued to heal at this supernatural rate as the swelling went down, color returned to normal, and mental behavior went from the bizarre to normal—every day was a miracle. There were other patients in the hospital with head injuries, seemingly not nearly as serious as Julie's, who had been there six months or more. Many of them were just learning how to walk and talk again.

During the next few days, we saw Julie protected by Jesus while He was accomplishing her healing. It was as if her body was left on the hospital bed to go through the healing while Julie herself—her soul maybe, for sure her spirit—seemed to retreat inside to be cuddled by Jesus until the healing process was complete. For the first several days after the accident we could not recognize anything about her that reminded us of our Julie. Then a little at a time we saw her return until she was totally back to normal. We could almost see the healing taking place before our very eyes. The nurses were amazed. They all called her their "miracle girl."

Even our hardcore neurosurgeon—without giving credit to God—said that her recovery couldn't be explained. He saw us praying and standing and believing day after day, and because of the results before his very eyes, he could not very easily have gone home and called us a bunch of kooks.

On the night of the accident we had been told that in addition to the brain damage, there would be considerable loss of hearing, since the mastoid bone had been part of the skull fracture. They were also quite sure that the optic nerve had been damaged—which we were told would cause either total, or at least partial, loss of eyesight. When Julie was dismissed only nine days after entering the hospital, the only outward sign of the accident was that her right eye was still a little bloodshot. She went home with no brain damage and no loss of eyesight (twenty-twenty vision). On the day of her release, however, the attending physician—even after watching her miraculous recovery—still insisted, "There will be a hearing loss," and he instructed us to take her to the audiologist in July. We did that, only to be told that she had perfect hearing. We thank Jesus for what He did on the cross for each one of us and for His wonderful promises in Psalm 91.

Author's Note: Julie and her husband, Rocky, live in San Antonio, Texas, where she works as a dental hygienist.

RENE HOOD

My testimony begins in July 1998. At this point in my life, I had eaten almost nothing for approximately two months, yet I continued to gain weight. I could not go outside in the direct sunlight for any length of time without my face becoming irritated to the point that if you placed your hand on my face, the print of your hand would remain there. I had also begun to develop black spots on my face, arms, and legs. Later, a red rash appeared on my face and throughout my body. Bruises would appear without my falling or having been hit.

During the month of July, my energy level was so low it was a challenge to just clean the bathtub after bathing. My body became racked with pain, even when I tried performing a task as simple as brushing my teeth. One particular night is still fresh in my memory. For the previous week or so, I had been choking when I'd lie down at night. This night was the same, but when I got up that morning, I made the shocking discovery I couldn't perform normal bodily functions. Knowing something had to be done quickly, I called my doctor early that morning. After his examination he referred me to Scott and White Hospital to see Dr. Nichols, a nephrologist.

The night prior to my seeing Dr. Nichols, my body aches had reached a new level; it became a norm for me to have a fever of 103 degrees or more. I felt like my brain was frying. I would lie on my bathroom floor in misery. My brown body transformed before my eyes into a gray color, covered with perspiration and rolled up in a fetal position. I told the Lord it would be so easy to give up the ghost and just go home to be with Him, but I said, "Lord, I know You are not finished with me. Lord, I hurt so badly and yet I know there are people out there You have called me to touch. My kids need me! I know I am walking in the *valley of the shadow of death, but I will fear no evil.* You promised me, Lord, in Psalm 91 that *only with my eyes would I see the reward of the wicked—that a thousand would fall at my side and ten thousand at my right hand, but it would not come nigh me.*"

My eighteen-year-old daughter took me to Temple Hospital. I was so weak I could barely walk. After a twenty-five-minute examination, the nephrologist, with no bedside manner and no sense of caring, said, "You are in the last stages of lupus and are going to die. I give you three months, and you will just go *poop.*" I was very angry he would speak such words to me in the presence of my daughter, without any sensitivity. Then he said, "It will not be easy because you will be in a lot of pain, but [as he pointed to my daughter] she's big enough—she can take care of herself." Then he walked out the door. I looked at my daughter and assured her, "Mom is not going anywhere."

I was hospitalized, running a high fever and unable to eat. I would have involuntary shakes I couldn't control, and my right lung had collapsed because of the mass of protein my kidneys were now throwing into my system. I looked like a seven-month pregnant woman. My kidneys were shutting down, my joints ached and were swollen, and the doctors had found a mass on my liver. After twelve days of their making one mistake after another and causing me more suffering without my getting any better, I asked my daughter to help me dress and take me back home to Bangs, Texas, because God was going to give me a miracle.

I am a living testimony of God's faithfulness to His promises. I went to my parents' house, where I would sit up and walk as well as I could, reminding God of what He had promised—"You will not be afraid of the deadly pestilence. It will not approach you."

My local doctor would call and remind me that those specialists said I was dying and I needed to be in a hospital. I wouldn't! I couldn't! I knew—"*Greater was He that was in me than he that was in the world.*" I had a supernatural peace I was well and the healing would manifest itself soon—so I kept pressing.

Since I would not go back to the hospital, and my condition, by sight, was no better, my doctor encouraged me to go to a nephrologist in Abilene, Texas. I finally agreed but refused the medicine because of the side effects. Not one doctor gave me one ounce of hope, but I was determined to receive the healing Christ had provided. *Then the miracle very slowly began to manifest.*

It was during those next few months I gradually started feeling better, and my strength started returning—slowly but surely. Finally, after I had been seeing the Abilene doctor for two months and once again being put through a battery of tests, he stated, "I'm looking at your paperwork, and I'm looking at you. If you had let us do what we wanted to do—and you wouldn't—we doctors would be patting ourselves on the back, saying we had gotten you in remission. All I can say is—whatever you have been doing, just keep doing it." Then he told me I was a *miracle*.

My doctor had a liver specialist meet me at the Brownwood hospital, and after a CAT scan and two sonograms, he could not find any mass in my liver. I was then sent to a blood specialist, and after reading the reports he repeated twice that I was *a wonder*. I have seen many Christmases since being told I would not even live to see that 1998 Christmas.

Radio program in Philippines

Rene ministering in the Philippines

Rene with Pastor Malou Causing

My prison ministry didn't suffer, and souls continue to be saved, delivered, and set free because I abided in God's Word and trusted Him to be faithful. I expect to have a book out soon called *Being Found in His Word.* We all need to be in His Word, refusing, no matter what, to be driven from His promises. I know this battle and subsequent victory give honor to a *faithful, loving, and caring God* who desires to be embraced by each one of us.

CHRYSTAL SMITH

It all began New Year's Eve night. I was convinced by the precipitation falling from the sky that driving forty-five to seventy minutes was risky, and besides, the Holy Spirit lives in me, so we can celebrate God and bring in the New Year anywhere, right? It was a battle of flesh and spirit, but the flesh was going to win without much of a fight. However, my Spirit-filled friend Tamara was dialing up God on one of her channels with a different message, so I decided to go.

It was a long drive, but we made it. We had already told a family we would stay with them through the morning of New Year's, so we continued on, lighting fireworks as the clock tolled 2009. The next morning came, and I was up fixing my bed and preparing for the trip home when the hostess of the house, Teresa, decided to share a book with me. She said, "Check this book out; it has a lot of wonderful testimonies in it that you might enjoy." She passed me the book and went back downstairs.

Later I joined everyone at the table, and she asked what I thought of the book. I replied, "I like it. It's truly a page-turner. I was wondering if I could take it with me?" Of course she granted me the privilege, and the rest of the week I would become consumed by the power of the Word of God and the reassurance of His deity in every testimony.

Chrystal Smith with a friend in front of a church in Germany

I returned to work after the holiday, and we sat in a morning staff meeting around the boss's desk and ran through the calendar and other administrative things we all had to attend to over the course of the next few weeks. As the meeting dragged on, a feeling of despair overcame me. Everything within me wanted to quit suddenly. I wondered what my purpose in this land of Germany was. I thought of all of the other things I could do for the kingdom of God somewhere else. I wanted to cry, but I had to hold it together because just breaking down in a staff meeting would be the grounds to start the psycho study on me.

Thankfully the meeting ended shortly thereafter, and I thought walking it off was a wise move. I stood at my desk wavering between going for a bite to eat or going to check my mail. After speaking this out loud to my colleague, I decided the walk to the post office was longer, and I needed the walk.

With my new book in hand, I walked and read slowly through the snow and ice, crossing streets and walking through car-filled parking lots to the post office, looking up slightly to check traffic at the street crossings, and more so to ponder the words of the testimony of Staff Sgt. Heath Adams and how it related to the verse of Scripture the author was explaining. I looked up in wonder trying to grasp how this guy received this gunshot wound, but I put my head right back down and continued my course through the busy post office parking lot.

As I neared the door, unconcerned about the possible danger associated with reading and walking in traffic over iced pavement while wearing the slipperiest shoes I own, I heard a voice call out, "Hey, ma'am, are you reading *Psalm 91*?" As I looked up, I thought, "Who could be interrupting me? Don't they realize I'm reading?" Once I responded yes, a tall blonde said, "Do you want to meet the author? She's right here."

As she informed the author that someone was reading her book, I was overcome with hysterical, joyous laughter and realized that God heard me in that moment in the earlier staff meeting.

Peggy Joyce Ruth, Leslie King, and Angie Schum stood before me telling me of their stay in Germany. I shared how I got a copy of the book, and we all laughed and talked in fellowship as I tried to gather myself. But I couldn't get past God and how He caused us to meet at that moment.

While we stood there, they shared with me their goal of visiting Landstuhl Regional Medical Center. They had come this long way in faith that they would actually get to touch the wounded and pray and lay hands on and even lead a soul to Christ. I didn't know how I could help them, but I was so compelled to do so. I returned to my office, and the rest of the afternoon was seemingly a wash for completing a large amount of work. I was working the phones for the kingdom of God. I called Ramstein Public Affairs to get a number to LRMC Public Affairs. They referred me to the protocol office at LRMC, who referred me back to LRMC PA. But of course by the time I redialed the number, they were gone for the day; their offices are within whisper room of the other. I then reached out to our chaplaincy. The administrative assistant Sabrina didn't have immediate answers, but she said she would get them. "Let me call you back," she said.

In the meantime I searched the Internet to see if there was a number, but all I could find was a press release about their Warrior Care Center. I also called the cell phone number on the business card Angie had given me earlier, only to get a guy named Scott who shared with me the extreme hope of the team from Brownwood, Texas. "Landstuhl is one of their main prayer focuses, so they would really like to be able to get in tomorrow," he said. He gave me the number to the other cell phone to reach Leslie. And while I spoke to Scott and then Leslie, I was convinced that they would get in. I just needed to make sure they had a point of contact when they got there.

I tried to make a couple more phone calls before Sabrina finally rang my line. Good news; she had some good numbers, but it was well after 4:30 p.m. The possibility of my getting the chaplain's assistant, whose name was associated with that line, was looking slim. And with no surprise, I didn't get the assistant. Instead I got the man in charge, Chaplain (Colonel) Griffith, who was willing to receive them the next day, but he offered no confirmation that they would be able to see the soldiers in the hospital. "Even celebrities don't get to go in there when they visit. I can show them the WCC, but getting into the hospital may be a problem." When they arrived at the hospital, Colonel Griffith showed them all over the hospital but said that civilians were not allowed in the hospital rooms. But, as only God can do, he finally said, "I don't know why I am doing this, but I'm going to give you permission to visit the wounded soldiers." What an awesome God we serve.

STORIES
FROM MEN and
WOMEN in UNIFORM

JOHN MARION WALKER

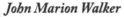

John Marion Walker
Army Air Corps Private 4th Class Specialist
35th Air Group, 21st Pursuit Squadron
Survivor of the Bataan Death March

We all remember the brutal attack on December 7, 1941, when Japanese torpedo bombers devastated U.S. Navy ships stationed at Pearl Harbor in the Hawaiian Islands, crippling almost every ship and airplane in the U.S. Pacific Fleet and giving Japan temporary control of the Pacific. This initiated America's involvement in World War II.

What many Americans do not remember, however, is that on the very same day of the attack on Pearl Harbor, the Japanese dropped bombs on U.S. and Filipino troops stationed in the Philippines, destroying their planes as well as their airfields. Nichols Field in Manila was totally wiped out. With the U.S. air and naval fleet badly crippled in Pearl Harbor, it left the troops in the Philippines without aid. John Walker was among the Americans who had been sent to the Philippines, where he witnessed this attack. John had accepted Jesus as his Savior years before but was not walking closely with the Lord at the time of the war. He had an older brother back home, however, who was a pastor and who was standing firm and immovable in faith that his younger brother, John, would, in fact, return home from the war. John recalled numerous instances where he knew God had intervened on his behalf to save his life. (Thank God for family members who pray unwaveringly in their faith for the protection of loved ones.)

One of these divine interventions took place during that early attack at Manila. The U.S. troops were living in tents with their cots under bamboo thickets. John was lying on his cot while a buddy was digging a foxhole several feet away. "Three times he called my name," John recalled, "so on the third time I left my cot and walked over to see what my buddy needed. Surprisingly, he insisted he had not once called me.

And before we had time to finish our conversation, a bomb hit the very cot on which I had been lying. From that moment on I knew God was with me."

In spite of being terribly outnumbered, outgunned, and without adequate supplies, these troops fought courageously to hold off the Japanese to the bitter end, but they were ultimately overpowered. It was during these early days of war, when Japan attacked for no apparent reason, that hate for the Japanese started building in John's heart—a hate that grew increasingly until some fifty years later.

John remembers he was sent to Manila to handle the machine guns on P-40 aircraft, but instead he found himself using an M-1 rifle with the Filipino 77th Infantry on the front lines. Tokyo Rose aided the Japanese military by taunting and demoralizing the American troops via radio as she reminded them of their helpless situation and impending doom. According to John, some found her somewhat entertaining; to others, she was demoralizing. During this time, another fateful God intervention happened when John was told to drive a truck to the front lines. There were two trucks he could choose from—a right-hand drive and a left-hand drive. He got into the left-hand drive because he was accustomed to it. But something told him, "John, don't take this truck," so he turned off the motor and jumped into the other truck—a right-hand drive. As soon as he entered the highway, gunfire went through the left side of the truck, exactly where he would have been sitting had he taken the other truck. Again, John realized God had spared him a second time!

The troops were forced to use World War I guns and ammunition that half the time didn't even work. Only one of four grenades exploded, and six of seven mortar rounds detonated. Many times corroded shells would burst the barrels of cannons. On the other hand, the Japanese were constantly being resupplied with fresh troops, equipment, and food. Despite Japan's advantage, the American and Filipino troops continued to fight, notwithstanding the fact that for almost five months they lived on one-fourth rations, once a day. This extended conflict, against impossible odds, bought much needed time for the rebuilding of the Pacific Fleet for our U.S. offensive in the Pacific. But on April 3, 1942, the Japanese surrounded them, and, being weakened to the point of total exhaustion, these American and Filipino troops could no longer withstand the horrible onslaught of the enemy and were forced to surrender on April 9, 1942.

This was the largest single defeat of American armed forces in history, and it came, not from the wishes of the more than seventy-five thousand fighting soldiers who were ready to fight to the death, but from command orders, in some cases under threat of court martial for failure to comply. On April 10, seventy-five thousand prisoners were lined up four abreast and started on a sixty-mile forced march, which took place under the most brutal conditions imaginable. Today that march is referred to as the *Bataan Death March*. They marched day and night without stopping, with no food or water from the Japanese, in very humid 115-degree temperature. During this march, John's new boots were worn completely out, and he was barefoot for the remainder of his three-and-a-half-year imprisonment. They were never issued any more clothing, and before it was over, his clothes had actually rotted off his body.

The Japanese would drive alongside many of the troops, cutting off heads with their bayonets as they passed by. Some of the men were pushed in front of oncoming trucks—others were clubbed with the captor's gun butts. At night Filipino citizens would throw them stalks of sugar cane to chew on for strength. They also threw Poncit—a breadlike substance made of rice mixed with bees, pork, grasshoppers, and so forth. The prisoners would break off chunks and then pass it on when the guards weren't looking. If these Filipino citizens had been caught, they would have been killed. The march never stopped, but the men discovered they could walk in their sleep. At night the two guys on the outside would lock arms with the two in the middle and let them sleep—then when the guards were not watching, they would change places so the two men on the outside could get in the middle and sleep. As the miles dragged on, men fell like flies from exhaustion and were shot to death. If a fellow soldier attempted to help one of his fallen companions, he would be killed. Artesian wells along the way were flowing with water, but if a man made a run for the water, he was shot on the spot. John lost one hundred pounds during that march—from 165 pounds to 65 pounds—where he remained for the duration of his time as a POW.

When they arrived at San Fernando in Pangpanga, one hundred or more prisoners were packed into World War I–era railroad boxcars to be taken to Camp O'Donnell. John was one of the first to be loaded, so he was able to breathe by putting his nose up to a little crack in the side of the car. Many who were in the middle of the cars suffocated, and they died standing up because there was no room to fall. Conditions at Camp O'Donnell were even more unbearable than the march. Another thirty thousand of the men died from starvation, disease, unsanitary conditions, injuries sustained in the march, and the brutality of the Japanese guards at the camp. They were given one rice ball a day. There were only two water pipes in the camp, and the water was only turned on once a day, so approximately one hundred men died daily. The healthier men were put to work digging graves. Some of the very sick were buried alive, but those who refused to do the burying were shot. John said it was quite common to be talking to someone and have him just fall over dead in mid-sentence. John knew he had to get out of the camp to survive, so whenever the guards asked for volunteers for outside work, he would comply. But, with every passing day, hatred for the Japanese was growing stronger in John's heart.

On May 6, John was sent to Manila to build a bridge to replace one that the U.S. Marines had blown up during their retreat. The volunteers were stripped of all their clothing in the middle of town and made to swim back and forth across the river in the swift currents, pushing logs for the bridge as they swam. They wore armbands with a number and were threatened that if anyone escaped, the rest would be shot. Eventually one man came up missing, and the guard was told to shoot ten prisoners—five on each side of the missing man's number. John was the sixth person, and if any one of the five had been sick that day, John would have moved into his spot. They were made to watch as the ten men were shot to death. John remembered with pain when one brother watched as his twin was murdered.

After building other bridges and airstrips, John was transferred again, this time to Bilibid Prison in Manila. The next time he volunteered he was loaded onto a Japanese ship that the POWs called "Hell Ship." The conditions on that ship were far worse than the death march and the prison camps. On his particular ship about fourteen hundred prisoners were crammed into the cargo area where they sat with their knees pulled tightly to their chest to make room for them all to fit. For thirty-nine days they sat this way without being able to move. The men who died were put overboard. Because they were not marked as prison ships, Allied submarines sank many of these ships. John made it to Hong Kong, then to Formosa, and finally, to Tokyo.

It was on January 26, 1945, that John moved to his final destination: Prison Camp Wakasen. Barefoot and wearing only underwear, the men were forced to walk in hip-deep snow. Several of the men froze to death the first night. For seven months they worked in the lead and zinc mine as slave labor. One day a huge slab fell and pinned a guy's legs. Six men picked it up, and the others pulled him out; however, the next day when the six men tried to lift the slab, they couldn't budge it. During this time John had another of his many miraculous interventions by God that once again saved his life. He was sent down four to five flights in the underground mine to a section where there were no signals or escape routes. The mine caved in that day, and John began to tell God he didn't want to die—that if God would get him out, he would serve Him. Supernaturally, God showed John a ladder in this lower level that had not been there before, and all were able to make it to safety. When the guards insisted there was no way for them to have climbed out, John showed them the ladder. They quickly told him they didn't put it there, and John said, "I know. Jesus did!"

God was doing miracles for John, but all the while the devil was contending for his life by filling him with more and more hate. Once a Japanese guard stood him in a ditch filled with two feet of snow, then took a 6-inch by 6-inch timber and brutally struck him four times on his ear, rupturing the eardrum. There was so much hate in John by this time that he promised the man he would find him and kill him. As soon as the war was declared over, he took a forty-five-caliber automatic pistol with three clips and ran down to find the guard, but he was nowhere to be found. Instead of rejoicing that the war was over, all he could think about was retaliation. However, God had intervened again, keeping him from murdering this man.

After the second atomic bomb was dropped on Nagasaki, Americans began dropping food from B-29 planes in fifty-five-gallon drums. Once John found a box of twenty-four Snickers; he ate all twenty-four in one sitting. That was probably another time when God saved his life. Eating that many Snickers at one time, after being starved for more than three years, would normally have killed him. The war was finally over, but of the seventy-five thousand soldiers who started the death march from Bataan, only one in three survived to go home.

John married Carolyn Hardeman on February 14, 1947, and they had five children. Fifty years later, John felt a strong impression that he was supposed to go back to Japan and help build a church, but hate still consumed his heart. It was on that first trip, after the YWAM leader kept delaying the first work day, that Carolyn finally had a dream in which she was told that John would not be allowed to build a church until he repented for the hatred he carried in his heart. He couldn't bring himself to do that until God spoke to him and said, "You will either serve Me, or you will serve the devil." That got John's attention, and repentance began to come. John said, "Every time we went to Japan, the hate was still there. But each trip, little by little, the hatred began to fade." Then, on his last trip to Japan, he finally got what he wanted. He talked to an old man inside one of the churches he helped build and heard the apology for the wrong that had been done to him and to his other fellow Americans—an apology he had wanted so long to hear. It was then that the release came for John to ask forgiveness for the hate in his heart. From then on, whenever he saw a Japanese, he felt he was supposed to ask forgiveness for hating them all those years. Interestingly, it was an American Japanese man, George (Joe) Sakato, a Congressional Medal of Honor recipient who fought for America in Europe, who presented John his Purple Heart. Finally, after fifty years the hate was driven from his heart. John and his wife have now traveled to Japan four more times, staying ninety days each trip, giving their time to help build churches.

Author's interview with John Walker: "This is one of the most powerful testimonies I've heard on the transforming power of God to enable one to forgive his enemies. Since you went through years as a POW in World War II, you can speak from experience. What would you say to a military man who is struggling with unforgiveness because he is embittered by the enemies he fought and the men he watched die?"

John replied, "You have to turn it over to the Lord, because if you don't, unforgiveness will eat you alive. You have to turn those memories over to the Lord, and then He will lead you and protect you."

THE MIRACLE OF SEADRIFT, TEXAS
NOT ONE OF THEIR SOLDIERS DIED IN THE WAR

McCown Brothers

One of my most memorable and exciting experiences was when I recently had the privilege of speaking to some of the residents of Seadrift, Texas, and hearing them tell stories of God's magnificent protection over their soldiers during World War II. This is their story of the boys who went off to war and the families who stayed behind to pray for their safety. Joe Fred Coward, along with Hollis and Gerald McCown, said that they experienced miraculous protection during World War II, and they knew why. There was a group of mothers and friends in their hometown of Seadrift, Texas, who were fervently praying for their safety. Coward and the McCown brothers were among fifty-two soldiers whose photos were placed in a large picture frame at a church and prayed over daily until they returned. Everyone I interviewed was still excited to tell me, "All fifty-two came home!"

Seadrift, Texas, World War II Prayer Board

It was the Psalm 91 promise of protection that the prayer warriors prayed over those young men who were daily putting themselves in harm's way to protect their country. One of the intercessors said that God had them literally bombard heaven. And one by one, every Seadrift soldier returned safely from the battlefields of Europe, the South Pacific, and the Far East, in spite of the fact that hundreds of thousands of American lives were lost on those battlefronts.

I spoke with Lora Weaver, who was one of the faithful intercessors. Even though she has enjoyed many years on this earth, and her hearing is not what it used to be, she still remembers with joy the faith they experienced in knowing that God was going to answer their prayers as they stood on the Ninety-first Psalm. She said, "We read the passage every time we met. It promises: *God gives His angels charge over us*. God is awesome." Mary Wilson Neill was another of the intercessors who said that some twenty women attended those prayer meetings every day. You can imagine the impression it made on the people in Seadrift when every one of the young men in their town came home from the war.

Fanny Maude (Granny) McCown was quite a prayer warrior. Known as a Five-Star Mother for having all five sons in World War II, she could often be heard crying out through tears as she prayed out loud in the smokehouse for the protection of her boys.

Fanny Maude McCown

McCown brothers in front of smokehouse where their mother prayed for their safety

Scattered throughout the world, those young men blessed practically every branch of the service. Glen McCown was in the army and fought in the Pacific arena. Danger faced him every day of the war, as he had the perilous job of going into caves throughout the islands looking for Japanese. Eugene McCown served in the navy in the South Pacific and was a constant target while operating landing crafts to lay down ground troops. Milton actively served in the navy, as well, throughout the war.

Another of Fanny McCown's sons, Gerald, joined the air force and fought in Europe. He was sent overseas in the largest convoy to ever

Gerald McCown

cross the Atlantic Ocean, and they were forced to travel in total blackout at night to be undetected by the enemy. The night before "D Day" he saw General Eisenhower talking to pilots and wishing them good luck. He pointed to Eisenhower and told his buddies, "Something big is going to be happening tomorrow. Wait, and see!" That something big was the Normandy invasion! Within less than twenty-four hours of seeing the general, he was flying over the English Channel, and he remembers, "I had never seen as many ships and planes in all of my life—they literally covered the waters and the sky." Gerald also remembers vividly how a friend he met after arriving in Europe was fearful of what the next day would bring. Sure enough, his plane was hit, and the concussion from the explosion was so bad that it threw Gerald's plane up, and dirt actually came through the cracks in the floorboard. What a difference it might have made if that young man had had a praying church back home. During those perilous times, Gerald McCown experienced the protective hand of God on numerous occasions. Some of his vivid memories were of the times he helped drop supplies from an airplane to ground troops in England and France as he stood on top of a thick steel plate to avoid the bullets that came up through the bottom of the plane. Gerald said they would often fly behind enemy lines and drop supplies and food to General Patton and his ground troops to help keep them moving as rapidly as possible across Europe to stop the Nazi advancement.

Hollis McCown

Hollis McCown, another of Fanny's sons, is still living to tell how he never left the States, but he knew his job of servicing the planes to keep them in optimum shape for our fliers and refueling them for their important missions was a vital link in the success of the war. Her sixth son entered World War II after the declaration was signed, then later fought again in the Korean War. What a heritage Fanny Maude McCown and her family have left for their descendants.

Joe Fred Coward, stationed in the Philippines, remembered barely escaping death when, as he drove an open army truck, he felt *something* whiz by his head—so close that he said his hair turned up. Coward is still living and continues to thank God for the divine protection he knew he had received on an almost daily basis. Gratefully he said, "I felt privileged to have been raised in a church that believed the Word and in the power of prayer."

The incredible story of God's protection didn't end with World War II. Gerald's grandson, Sgt. Leslie King, served in Iraq. King has not only carried on the legacy of his grandfather and uncles, but the church in Seadrift has also continued in the famous heritage left to them.

Sgt. Leslie King

One day Sgt. King called his mother to say that something was not right. He didn't feel the shield of protection anymore for his men, and he knew something was badly amiss. It was at that time that the family noticed all the military pictures were gone from the bulletin board. They had been taken down because the actual *war* was considered to be over. (Little did anyone know the battles yet to be fought!) After bringing this to the attention of the pastor, the photos were put back. Interestingly, without knowing that his picture had been removed and subsequently put back on display, Sgt. King wrote home again to say that his peace and security had returned. They didn't lose any more men, and the troubles had begun to subside. The family knew that it was no coincidence that the deaths and trouble occurred within the three-week period when the photos were out of sight. Even though the troops were being prayed for, there was something about corporate prayer from an entire church, with the pictures displayed so the intercessors had visual contact when they prayed, that made a big difference. What a powerful tool prayer is!

JEFFERSON BASS ADAMS

Jefferson Bass Adams, 1st Sergeant, World War II
36th Division, Army
Tribute: A Family Love Story

Author's Note: With so many challenges to military marriages, I would like to give this tribute to JB and Francis Adams, parents of my good friend Kay Sheffield and grandparents to our precious daughter-in-law, Sloan. *This love story is an inspiration for all times and a family treasure.*

When JB and his two buddies, Allen and Skinny, were drafted into the service during World War II, they were sent to Florida for training. It was hard for these young men to leave their wives, knowing they would be separated for at least two years. However, those spunky eighteen-year-old wives had other plans. With one suitcase apiece, in a 1930s Plymouth that was barely travel worthy, they set out from Texas to follow their husbands. Once, when the car ran out of water, the resourceful threesome pulled off a hubcap, climbed a fence, and brought back hubcaps full of water from a pond and filled the radiator. In spite of head gasket problems in Mississippi and flat tires in the rain, nothing could stop them. They followed their guys through Florida, North and South Carolina, Virginia, and on into Massachusetts, locating the army bases and renting rooms in local boarding houses. Each time the guys were transferred, the girls were made to promise they would go immediately back home to Texas. However, no sooner would the guys find themselves at their new base than the girls would show up. Once, when the company was doing maneuvers at a new base, the guys looked up just in time to see the faithful old Plymouth come rolling by. Late that night when JB got off duty at 2:00 a.m. and located the boarding house where he was told the girls would be, he opened the door to find stairs and several closed doors at the top of the stairs. Just as he was pondering where Francis might be, a hand suddenly came out of one of the doors and simply pointed to a room where he found Francis waiting for him with what only a woman could bring in one suitcase. She was a *nester*. In that one suitcase she brought only two dresses in order to leave room for the tablecloth, curtains, two plates, and a flower vase to make each place a *home away from home*.

When finances got low, the girls simply found a job. At one of their temporary homes, they discovered that the huge bump in the road in front of their boarding house caused produce to bounce off the local farm truck every afternoon as it passed. The girls would sit on the porch, waiting to see what would fall. That would be their dinner. Like gypsies, they moved all over the United States throughout the men's training for overseas.

After being sent initially to Africa, JB was among the first American troops to hit the continent of Europe at the Salerno invasion in Italy. The war was fierce, but God was faithful to His promises. JB recalled three instances when God's protection was miraculous. The first was when JB's company was ready to cross the Rapido River that surrounded Monte Cassino, where the Germans were using the monastery on top of that mountain as an outpost. Three separate times the orders changed just five minutes before JB was to cross. Of the men who were sent across, 90 percent were killed—more than two thousand men. A second miraculous protection came when JB and a buddy were filling their canteens at a creek, and a bullet whizzed between them. In a third incidence, when his company was ready to move forward at Mt. Lungo, a herd of goats came out of nowhere, detonating the mines in the field they were about to cross. Not one man was killed crossing that field.

LIEUTENANT COLONEL BRIAN AND MEL BIRDWELL

When American Flight 77 crashed into the Pentagon on September 11, 2001, I was standing fifteen to twenty yards away from the point of impact. It took only a few seconds for my life to be changed forever. Searing second- and third-degree burns were inflicted over more than 60–70 percent of my body. I was unrecognizable by those who treated me, and some mistook me for dead.

However, God had another plan for my life, and no terrorist would be able to work against the purposes of God. My survival didn't happen by luck or mere chance. It happened because a sovereign God had a specific plan for me to live and not die. Had I remained in the office, I would have died. Had I left my office any sooner, I would have been in the path of the plane. Had I left any later, I would have been in the path of the plane. And while I do not understand why God chose to allow me to live when so many others perished, I do know that He was with me.

It was a day like any other at the Pentagon outside Washington DC. I had just stepped out of the men's room on the second floor. I took several steps and was in front of the first set of elevators when there was a sudden deafening explosion. It wasn't the usual sound of construction that I had been hearing from the remodeling in this section of the Pentagon. After seventeen years in the army, being a Gulf War veteran, and spending more than ten years as an artillery officer, I was familiar with loud explosions, forceful concussions, and other noises of war. But this was louder than anything I'd heard in my life. This was the sound of gnarling metal slamming its way through concrete, a scraping, screeching, high-pitched, thunderous blast.

Immediately everything went black, as if I had been thrown into a deep, dark cavern. An intense force blasted toward me. Fire exploded right at me and suddenly was all around, throwing me across the hall, ripping my glasses from my face, and then tossing me limply onto the floor. I could hear the sound of flying wreckage all around me. The ceiling panels and light fixtures crashed down, and the walls shook. But I couldn't see anything except for a ring of yellow surrounding me. Then I realized...I was on fire!

The heat was so intense that the polyester pants of my uniform melted into my legs. My arms, back, legs, face, and hair were alight with flames.

The thick smoke tightly enveloped me, suffocating me to the point that I had to breathe it in. I swallowed it as I gasped for air. I recognized the overpowering smell of jet fuel. I couldn't help but gulp it in and choked on the heavy vapors and the dust from the building debris as I struggled just to get oxygen.

It was hard to keep my eyes open due to the intense amount of smoke and heat. The fire stung my eyes and my body screamed in pain, but there was no way to put out the flames.

I tried to stand four or five times, using my hands and my arms to get up. I managed to get on one knee, and then I fell. My legs wouldn't support me, and I had no balance. The concussion had damaged my equilibrium. And because it was so black around me, I lost all sense of depth. I struggled to breathe. My lungs had been burned from the intense heat, and I had inhaled aerosolized fuel. I could taste the jet fuel in my mouth. I breathed in smoke, choking and coughing.

I tried desperately to see something—anything—other than the ring of fire surrounding me. But there was nothing. No wall, no doors, no elevator, nothing. It was as though there was nothing to touch except whatever I was lying on.

Finally the pain was too much to bear. I tried to stand up one last time and fell sideways. In anguish I screamed, "Jesus! I'm coming to see You!"

I knew I was going to die. As a soldier I'd been trained never to give up. But I did. I didn't try to get up again. Instead, I thought. "OK, Lord, if this is the end for me, if this is the way I am to die, then OK." I'd stopped moving and thought this was the end. I was still gasping for air; it felt as if I'd opened an oven door and was breathing in the hot air. Yet I had quit struggling—even though the fire and pain seared through my body. At that moment the building became absolutely quiet to me. I no longer heard the shrill, blaring sounds still screeching around me.

I lay on the floor and wondered when my soul would depart from my body—and what it would feel like. While I didn't know exactly what to expect, I knew it had to be better than what I was currently enduring. As I focused on eternity, I was enveloped by an absolute silence, an absolute peace...as if what was happening in the building wasn't really happening. I was separated from everything going on around me. God was in that place with me—it was just He and I. And while the pain was excruciating, I felt indescribable peace.

I wanted to see the light of that tunnel into eternity, which I'd heard so many people with near-death experiences discuss. So I waited. And waited. But the light never came. I lay there waiting, with my face toward the ground.

Suddenly, on the left side of my face, I felt something trickle past my eye and run down my cheek. It wasn't a huge gush, just a small stream. It wasn't warm, so I knew it wasn't blood. It was cold; it was water. Somehow I had landed under one of the working sprinkler systems, and the sprinkler began dousing the fire that was consuming me.

With the touch of water, everything changed. My courage was renewed to try to escape again. I opened my eyes. My face was pointed toward the ground. Immediately I was reoriented. The fire was out around me. "OK, I'm not dead yet," I thought, "so now I need to get medical attention—quickly." I knew now I had to move rapidly toward the light. I took a deep breath, coughed, and tried to get on my feet again. My survival instincts clicked on again, so I tried not to think about what I'd seen hanging from my arm.

I knew I had to walk straight down the closed corridor. Behind me was the point of impact; to my front, the fire door. To my left all the access doors were locked. To my right everything was still covered by the renovation plywood from the areas under construction. There was no escape. I had made it all the way to safety, only to find that there was no safety! I thought, "This can't be happening!" I knew my second chance at life was over. I was trapped and was now forced to wait helplessly for the rapidly approaching fire and smoke to catch up to me. I didn't know what I was going to do—and the smoke from the point of impact was rushing down the corridor, making it impossible to find any good air.

Then suddenly, unexpectedly, a locked door to the B Ring opened. Out came Colonel Roy Wallace, who stepped into the corridor to see if he could work his way around the building. From his startled look, I must have seemed ghastly. I was black from the burns and soot. Sections of my pants were either gone or had melted into my skin. The back of my shirt was completely gone; the front was still there and soaked in blood. And I was soaking wet from the sprinklers.

Next, Lieutenant Colonel Bill McKinnon stepped into the corridor. I recognized him immediately. Bill and I knew each other. It was a shock when I realized that I recognized Bill but he didn't recognize me. He couldn't recognize me, and my plastic nametag pinned to my uniform shirt was melted and covered with blood. But the whole time they were moving me I kept shouting to Bill, "Call Mel!" and then, "Put me down!" Six officers rushed toward me and began to pick me up. As they lifted me, the pain became unbearable. "Put me down! Put me down!" I yelled. "No, don't touch me! It hurts!" I grabbed Bill's shirt with my right hand and saw that my hand was bloody and shreds of skin were falling off my fingers. My arms were burned all the way up to my armpits. I felt cooked, like a hot dog that's been burnt. The inside may still be meaty, but the outside was blackened and hard. As I kept screaming for them to refrain from touching me, they grasped hands with each other underneath my back and legs. Chunks of flesh came off when they grasped my limbs.

My face was already puffing up, and I could feel the swelling. Most of my skin was gone. And what little was left was charred black. I looked down at my injuries and began to tremble severely. The manner of my death was filling my thoughts as I lay there. I was in shock. But my mind was still good and very active. I didn't feel that much pain anymore, probably because I was so concerned about how I was going to die. I wanted to die a dignified death in which I didn't panic.

About that time, a woman ran down the stairs to escape. But when she saw me lying there, she felt led to pray with me. By the look on her face when she saw my injuries, I was struck again by how serious my condition must be. She asked my name and then told me, "Brian, my name is Natalie. I feel the need to pray with you. Would that be all right?"

"Yes, please!" I couldn't believe a Christian was there beside me. Even more, she had thought to grab her Bible before she left her desk. My body was in shock. Then she began to read Psalm 91 to me:

He who dwells in the shelter of the Most High
Will abide in the shadow of the Almighty.
I will say to the LORD, "My refuge and my fortress;
My God, in whom I trust."

For it is He who delivers you from the snare of the trapper
And from the deadly pestilence.
He will cover you with His pinions,
And under His wings you may seek refuge;
His faithfulness is a shield and bulwark.

You will not be afraid of the terror by night,
Or of the arrow that flies by day;

Of the pestilence that stalks in darkness,
Or of the destruction that lays waste at noon.
A thousand may fall at your side,
And ten thousand at your right hand;
But it shall not approach you.
You will only look on with your eyes
And see the recompense of the wicked.

—Psalm 91:1–8

Natalie had just finished praying with me when Dr. Baxter let her know they were getting ready to move me. Within minutes of arriving at that area, I was prepped for the hospital. Once the *golf-cart-sized Pentagon ambulance* arrived, they brought over a gurney. "Please don't forget to call my wife!" I shouted to Natalie. "I won't forget," she said back.

The driver dropped me off to wait for an official ambulance or medevac helicopter. And there I lay, helpless, with the sun from the bright, cloudless morning sky beating down on my already cooked face. I was grateful when a woman came and held an umbrella over me to shield me from the sun.

As I lay on that gurney, unable to move, in incredible pain, time seemed to stop. I wondered, "What's taking so long?" Everything up to that point had gone so quickly. Medical officers had rushed to take care of me, and then I'd been quickly taken out to the parking lot. "So why am I waiting here? Shouldn't someone be rushing me to the hospital by now?" I thought.

I couldn't see much of the scene taking place outside, but I could hear it. There was still chaos. Thousands of people streamed out into the north parking area. Sirens blared; people screamed and cried. Then some police officers or some authority figures began announcing, "There's another plane coming! Get away from the building!" I heard the word "plane," and everything sunk in. The explosion and my lying out on the gurney near death were connected to the World Trade Center plane crashes that I'd watched on television with my co-workers before I left for the men's room.

When people heard the warning, some started to scream, and the person holding the umbrella over me threw the umbrella aside and took off running. I wanted to run too—but I couldn't even move.

Just then Natalie emerged from another side of the building. Somehow she spotted my stretcher and immediately came to me. She began to pray with me once again, encouraging me. I could hear all the chaos around as people ran for cover. While medics were working on me with the IV and evaluating the level of my injuries, I paid attention to Natalie; I didn't concentrate on what the others were doing to me.

Immediately I was struck by how serious my condition must be. Since I was the first person evacuated, I knew from experience that meant I was the one in the worst shape.

Aerial view of the Pentagon following the terrorist attack of 9-11

I heard a lot of sirens going by, but no vehicle stopped to pick me up. Finally Natalie and a few other people decided to move me closer to the road for better access to an ambulance. I was loaded and reloaded into vehicles commandeered since no ambulance or helicopter arrived. God had just the right one in Army Captain Wineland, who was flagged down in his SUV and told "Your service is demanded. You're going to drive him to the hospital." Two hours later, Natalie's husband, Mark, was able to get through to Mel. "Your husband is alive!" Dr. Williams, the trauma surgeon, called to tell Mel the extent of the injuries, and then the nurse called, "You've got to get here now!" The traffic was in gridlock all over the city.

God was faithful through the many miraculous events as the medical personnel in ER primarily worked to secure the airway passage so that it did not close off. The medics began fluid resuscitation as the FAA opened up airspace to medevac me to a burn unit. A CAT scan revealed no broken bones, even though I had suffered the initial force of the explosion. I survived even though they had told my wife that my death was imminent within seventy-two hours.

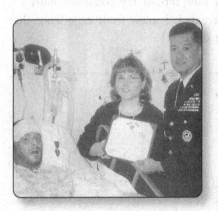

(L) Brian and Mel when Brian is presented a Purple Heart for wounds sustained on September 11, 2001, by then Chief of Staff of the Army General (Ret.) Eric K. Shinseki. (R) Brian administers the oath of reenlistment to SGT Bigelow, October 16, 2001.

* * *

Instead of tragic news, on September 13, Mel's cell phone rang. It was the Secret Service. They were calling on behalf of the president. This was the first clue as to what an absolutely godly man we were dealing with. They were asking for permission to visit that day. At around 11:00 a.m., President and Mrs. Bush arrived. They first visited two other Pentagon casualties on the third floor, then walked the flight of stairs to the burn unit ICU. For the president's visit to the seven patients and their families there was no media, no photo ops.

A nurse stepped into the room and said, "They're on their way." Several members of the burn unit staff came into the room with us—they wanted to see the president too. Mrs. Bush entered first and said, "Colonel Birdwell, it's nice to meet you. We're really proud of you, and you're an American hero."

Mel had to interpret for me. I could only mouth things since I had tubes in my mouth and nose. Either that, or I would spell words in the air with my finger.

"Where are you from?" Mrs. Bush asked.

"He's from Fort Worth," Mel was able to answer for me.

First Lady Laura Bush, President Bush, and Brian share a "Texas moment" at the White House prior to the Concert for America, September 9, 2002.

She perked right up. "Really? I'm from Midland, Texas!" And she did that little "Texas happy dance" that Texans do when they meet one another.

After asking about the family with Mel, Mrs. Bush said, "Well, Colonel Birdwell, I brought someone to see you."

* * *

Mel remembered it more vividly: The president comes into Brian's room, and he walked to the foot of Brian's bed. His eyes were bloodshot, and you could tell his visit here was gut-wrenchingly difficult for him. He simply said, "Colonel Birdwell." Brian's eyes were huge; he didn't even blink as he took all this in. Then the president *saluted* Brian!

Brian's arms were wrapped in sterile towels at this point, because he was about to go into surgery. But the president saw that Brian was actually trying to *return* his salute! Brian lifted his arm—and it's kind of like he's in slow motion at this point because bending his arm is just hideously painful. All the president could see was just muscles; all the flesh was gone. Brian got his arm about three quarters of the way up, and the president just stood there holding his salute the entire time, with tears in his eyes, while Brian finished his own salute. The president honored Brian, because it's the junior officer who salutes first and holds it, not the senior officer.

President Bush and Brian exchange salutes in the diplomatic reception area at the White House, September 9, 2002.

President Bush then said, "Colonel Birdwell, you're a great American, a hero, and we are going to get the guys who did this. This will not go unanswered." After that, the president asked, "Mrs. Birdwell, may we pray for your family?"

"Yes, please!" I answered. "We'd really appreciate that." Soon after, one of the Secret Service agents stepped into the room. It was time for the president to move to the next family, the last burn victim. So they said good-bye and went to the next room. After that, the nurse kicked everyone out of the room to prep Brian for surgery.

***

When General Van Antwerp visited, I was alert enough to remember he was there. When I saw him, I asked about my co-workers Cheryle Sincock and Sandi Taylor. The general paused and then shook his head mournfully. They were gone. Gone.

That one word exploded inside my head. I hit my head against the pillow and groaned. I didn't think I could feel worse pain than what I'd experienced up to this point. I was wrong. Knowing my co-workers were dead was worse than any of the burns or treatments I'd experienced. Cheryle and Sandi were dead, and I was alive. A trip to the bathroom had saved my life.

"Oh, God!" I cried to myself. I didn't know where Cheryle and Sandi had stood with God. I had never spoken with them about where they stood with Jesus. How I wished I could have one more conversation with my co-workers. I vowed that if I survived, I would never live with another regret of having not shared my faith. I would never again give up an opportunity to tell someone about Jesus. I couldn't go back and witness to Cheryle and Sandi. But I could become more intentional about discussing faith with others from this point forward.

Many miracles rose from the ashes. There is no real reason for me to be alive, except God. I was only fifteen to twenty yards from the point of impact. That's two car-lengths! I know things would have been very grim if I hadn't had God protecting me that day. His plan for me was finely detailed, from a trip to the men's room to Natalie Olgetree's prayers and proclaiming of scriptures—all for God's glory. I may not have known what the next step was, but He did. God had a great plan for me, and He sent just the right people who would be able to help me survive.[1]

NATALIE OGLETREE

Who would have known that after only having been an employee at the Pentagon for eight weeks, something would happen in this short span of time that would cause Natalie Ogletree to be remembered forever. On 9/11, when the plane smashed into the building, she was at her job as a financial manager for the navy on the fifth floor in the adjacent wedge of the impact. Since the ceiling in front of her office had collapsed, she and co-workers were directed to an emergency exit route at the rear of the office. She gathered up her things and started for an exit. Thinking they were trapped, one can only imagine their relief when they finally found the fire escape that delivered them straight to the ground floor. The adjacent wedge was actually empty, eerie like a ghost town. It was a miracle that the plane hit one wedge of the Pentagon that had been remodeled and strengthened—or the plane probably would have traveled much farther into the building if it had struck in any other wedge. This new construction area of the Pentagon had been reinforced.

When the group of about twenty-five co-workers arrived at the first floor, military personnel were desperately running to the impact site, retrieving wounded persons, and bringing them to a secure area where they could be laid on the floor and their injuries could be attended to. Natalie was on her way out of the building with her co-workers when she came across a military man who was being carried by several men. When she looked over, something told her to let her group go on and for her to return to this particular man. He was severely injured with burns over 60 percent of his body, but he was not dead. However, his body looked not only burned but injured as well. As a child, Natalie had fallen into a bucket of hot water that her mom was using to mop the floor, so she knew what it was like to have burns from her knees to her shoulders. She still had scars and could remember the pain.

The man's shoes had blown off, his socks were gone, his arms and face were burned, and his whole body was smoky and charred. He was screaming for relief from the pain. She ran to his side, and he asked Natalie to make sure she would call his wife, Mel, and tell her he was OK. Every indication was that he was not going to make it, so Natalie listened carefully to the words to give to his wife. Several times it appeared that he was slipping away because the pain and injuries were so severe.

As the military performed triage on him, Natalie held his hand and prayed with him, trying to get his mind off the pain. She began to quote the Lord's Prayer and Psalm 23. However, there was a psalm that three weeks before, her mother, Delores Green, had told her about—Psalm 91. In fact, her mother had asked Natalie to pray it every morning. She was glad that she had grabbed her Bible that was lying on her desk beside her purse in the haste. Natalie did not know the psalm by heart, but two flips and she was there. She began to read the words.

"He who dwells in the shelter of the Most High will abide under the shadow of the Almighty...!" She began to declare Psalm 91 over him. She would later find out the injured man was Colonel Brian Birdwell. Colonel Birdwell's arms were bloody and his feet were still smoking but she read this psalm of protection over him. Then she would return to Psalm 23, which she knew by heart, and would quote it with him and they would pray the Lord's Prayer. Then back to Psalm 91. For thirty to thirty-five minutes she went back and forth at least seven times reading the psalm over him. Something supernatural was taking place in him.

Brian and Mel with the Ogletree family—Natalie, Mark, Avery, and Aaron. Natalie prayed over Brian in the hallway of the Pentagon as he was being triaged on 9/11.

She prayed with him one more time and told him, "You are going to be OK!" She exited, but God was still not finished. Once she was out of the building, she ran into him again and could see the extent of his injuries, so she prayed once again. There were no ambulances that could make it into the Pentagon, so those in charge were trying to wave down civilians to transport the injured. They loaded him into a small SUV, but it was not large enough, and they took him back out again. Only a few vehicles behind that car was an army captain in a Ford Expedition who took him to Georgetown University Hospital. Natalie continued to pray. She had done everything she knew to do in the natural, and it didn't look good, but she had activated the supernatural power of God's Word over him. For two months she searched for any information about him and kept her church and her Bible study praying for him. Then, on December 2 or 3, she heard on the news about a survivor's miraculous story—and she began to cry, knowing in her heart that it was Mr. Birdwell. Later the next spring, Natalie would meet someone in the Pentagon who asked her if she had met someone on September 11. The gentlemen informed her, "Brian is looking for you!" Natalie and her family (Mark, Avery, and Aaron) would eventually meet LTC Brian Birdwell, his wife, Mel, and their son, Matthew. It was not until the anniversary of the Pentagon attack that she realized that the date 9/11 was just like the psalm she had read.

Natalie's mother had been very timely in telling her daughter about Psalm 91 just three weeks before this tragic event. And in this traumatic situation, Natalie grabbed her Bible as she left the office and read the promises of Psalm 91 over Brian Birdwell for over half an hour. When Colonel Birdwell needed the encouragement to keep fighting to live, it wasn't his military training that kicked in—it was the prayers and the Word that Natalie Ogletree brought to him that fateful moment.

JOSH STOVALL

Christmas of 2005, our son had just finished boot camp and training school and had been sent to his permanent duty station in Fairbanks, Alaska. We all knew when he entered the army that he would be heading to Iraq sometime after the training was over. I never dreamed that at Christmas that year I would be faced with knowing when he got back on a plane heading to Fairbanks, he would do an almost immediate turnaround to El Paso for two weeks, and then be off to Iraq before the end of January. My fears and concerns were escalated because he was a cavalry scout—the one who purposely seeks out the enemy. As a former military person myself, and coming from a long line of military families, I knew the risks when he signed up, but he was totally dedicated to the cause; he always told me, "Don't worry, Mom; I know what I'm doing."

He got to fly home that Christmas and had already been told he would deploy sometime in January once they returned to Alaska, so that Christmas was filled with trying to get as much time in as possible, be positive, and tell him all the things that were weighing on my heart. Gift giving was heart wrenching. He had told me to please make sure any gifts were small enough to put in his gunnysack; otherwise, he would just have to store them at home.

215

While shopping for him I looked at potential gifts, thinking, "How can I tie this gift to home or to our love?" So I did things like purchasing a compass and putting notes on each item with sayings such as—"This compass will point you in the right direction while there, but it will also point you in the direction of home."

Due to weather, we were not sure he was going to get out of the Seattle airport (a layover from Fairbanks to Dallas). Because of the delay, he missed his flight into Brownwood, but we didn't know that until we were standing at the airport gate. It was heart wrenching as one by one the passengers got off, with NO JOSH to be seen. I think I even asked them to go look to make sure (he is 6'4" and weighs 250 pounds), and it was only a nineteen-passenger plane. I don't typically cry, but I stood in that airport crying like a baby because the delay meant less time with him than had been planned.

My husband drove to Dallas so Josh did not have to wait until five the next evening to get a plane home. I think God was involved with the flight delays, because while I was waiting for them to get back to Brownwood, I remembered a medallion Josh had given me when I was going through a tough patch in my life. When he got here, I had put the medallion in wrapping paper and taped it to his bathroom mirror. It has praying hands on one side and a quote on the other: "I said a prayer for you today...I know He answered." After he opened it, he said that he did not want to talk about or think about his impending deployment the rest of his Christmas leave. When he gave it to me, he had said, "You have to give this back to me when you no longer need it." So I enclosed those same words to him along with the medallion. While he was deployed, I asked him constantly if he was carrying the medallion. He would say, "Yep, got it in my wallet." I am happy to say that my son handed me the medallion earlier this summer.

A friend of mine, Ann Johnson, had gotten me a couple of copies of Peggy Joyce Ruth's book *Psalm 91* for military families. She had also printed me a copy of the Psalm 91 verse she had stored on her computer. At that time, I did not attend church or practice my beliefs often, but I clung to that promise from God for His protection of my son. I did not know it then, but God put it on my heart to make that verse a living, breathing brace to hang on to over the course of the next eleven months. He was supposed to return in February 2006; however, his was the first unit to be extended by several months, so he had to stay until November 2006. That verse is also what I now realize was the starting of God pulling my family and me closer to Him. I can say today that I am a church-attending, belief-practicing Christian.

For Christmas, I printed enough copies of the Psalm 91 verse for my entire family (about fifteen adults) on beautiful paper, rolled the copies, tied them with a pretty ribbon, and placed them on the Christmas tree.

When all the extended family arrived, I told them of the power of that verse and asked that they each place their copy somewhere that would allow them to pray that verse daily over Josh while he was deployed. I personally had mine in a frame on my desk at work, and I prayed it daily.

I also prayed it when I was feeling worried or anxious about him. I had Josh promise to pray it before he *broke wire* each day. While writing this, I went back and reread some of the e-mails he had written me. This is a quote from one of them: "Every time I am about to break wire for the first time of the day, I pull out the Bible and read Psalm 91. I promised you that, and I am doing as I said. Sergeant tells me to put it away sometimes, and I just keep on driving and doing what I must."

In his very first e-mail from Iraq he said, "When military finishes a radio transmission, they use the word *out*," so to signify that Psalm 91 was going to get him out of Iraq alive we each signed our e-mails and letters with "91 out" beneath our names. *When Josh returned from Iraq, he had a tattoo placed on his calf—"91 Out."*

ANDREW WOMMACK

Andrew Wommack
Specialist, First Class, Vietnam

My deployment in Vietnam was from January 1970 through the end of February 1971, serving in the 196th Infantry Brigade as an assistant to the chaplain. I was well aware of the security God had provided through His protection covenant of Psalm 91, and I knew it was just as reliable in wartime as in peacetime, but I also knew it needed to be seriously appropriated by faith in this new hostile environment. I will be sharing four instances that immediately come to mind in regard to God's faithfulness to this Psalm 91 covenant of protection.

It was against regulations to leave the military base at brigade level without going in a convoy with an armored personnel carrier before and behind. My captain, however, was a chaplain, and chaplains could do pretty much what they wanted to do. One day he wanted to go out in the countryside to visit a Vietnamese pastor. Against regulations, I got a jeep out of the motor pool, and we got off the main highway and drove out of the area to find this man. Since it was against regulations, it was more than a bit risky—here was an American jeep and two American soldiers out in the midst of Vietnam with no protection around. After visiting with the pastor for about thirty minutes or so, the chaplain asked him, "Is there any Viet Cong activity around here?" The pastor assured him there was a great deal of Viet Cong activity. He had us look out the window to a long building directly across the street, which he said was a Viet Cong headquarters. Needless to say, there were Viet Congs walking around with AK-47s—the Russian-made weapon. They were not American friendly, and they were right across the street with our jeep in plain sight. The chaplain got so scared that all he wanted was to get out of there as quickly as possible. There we were—two Americans in uniform, in an army jeep, driving through these Vietnamese guards who had AK-47s on their shoulders. We know they saw us because as we drove they would get out of the way of the jeep and let us pass. They didn't say a thing to us, and they never pointed a weapon at us as we drove right through the midst of them. There were probably about six of them, and they simply parted as we drove on by. The whole thing was so incomprehensible that the chaplain and I just looked at each other, speechless. I'm not sure what happened. There is no telling what God did to cause us to be able to get out of there alive. There is no natural explanation for those Viet Congs not to have taken us captive or killed us on the spot. "He will cover you with His pinions [feathers], and under His wings you may seek refuge; His faithfulness is a shield" (Ps. 91:4).

Another time, I was driving from Da Nang to my headquarters some sixty miles south. It was a paved highway that went north and south through Vietnam. Sometimes people drove alone, but it was against regulations and was especially dangerous when one drove through towns because there were people everywhere. You were forced to slow down almost to a stop with this sea of people around your vehicle, and it was not uncommon for one of them to wrap a cloth around a hand grenade, pull the pin, and throw it into the gas tank. The gas would eat the rag away, releasing the handle and blowing up the gas tank. I had been a little apprehensive about getting through, so my faith was just a little shaky. I specifically remember going across a huge bridge right outside of the town, because I remember I was praying and singing praises to God for His divine protection in getting me through safely. I also remember hearing a lot of gunfire, but I didn't think much about it because gunfire was quite common. That was just something you learned to live with. But then as I continued south on Highway One, in less than ten minutes after crossing the bridge, I saw a convoy and another chaplain's assistant who was a friend of mine going north. I waved at him and went on. Later I met this same guy in Da Nang, and he said, "How did you get across the bridge right outside that town?" I said, "I just drove across it. Why?" Then he told me that by the time they got to the bridge, less than ten minutes after I had crossed it, the convoy was stopped because of all the Vietnamese and American bodies they had piled up that had been killed. It turned out the Viet Congs had been on one side of the bridge, the Americans on the other side, and while I was just singing and worshiping the Lord, I had driven over the bridge, right through the middle of the firefight. I was totally unaware I was driving through a huge gunfire battle, and I never got touched. "A thousand may fall at your side and ten thousand at your right hand, but it shall not approach you" (Ps. 91:7).

Another supernatural protection came when I was with 120 other men on a landing zone located about forty-five miles from the nearest U.S. emplacement. I was asleep one night while some of our guys were practice-firing from a U.S. Huey helicopter. They had asked for grid coordinates but had gotten the wrong grid cord, so this Huey Cobra began firing on our hill. A fifty-caliber machine gun was shot at our bunker—made of two layers of four-by-twelves on top and two layers of sand bags—and those caliber rounds went through our bunker right beside my bed. I narrowly escaped being killed by friendly fire that night, yet when I woke up the next morning, I didn't know anything had happened. When we looked, however, we could see where the bullets had come through the bunker. Several people on our hill were killed from that accident, and it came within a few feet of me, but none of it touched me. "[I] will not be afraid of the arrow [bullets] . . . [they] shall not approach [me]" (Ps. 91:5–7).

Another time when I pulled bunker duty on landing zone (LZ) west, there was a bunker out on a finger of that 441-meter-tall hill. It was so steep that this hill was almost impregnable, except for one way you could come up, and that was where this bunker was located. It was sort of an outpost, and I was down there with three other guys pulling bunker guard. I pulled the first guard duty, and there was a guy who sat up on top with me. He was a Puerto Rican who had been drafted and didn't speak any English. I tried talking to him, and all he would say was, "Forty days." I asked, "Have you been in the country forty days?" He would simply say, "Forty days." I couldn't talk to him, so I pulled my four-hour bunker guard, and then I lay on top of the bunker and went to sleep. We're supposed to stay there until six, but when I woke up about three or four in the morning, everyone was gone. I didn't know what had happened, so I finished up the bunker guard until six o'clock and then headed up the hill. The chaplain met me and asked if I was all right or if I had been hurt, and I said, "What are you talking about?" It turned out while I was sleeping right beside this Puerto Rican, he had gone crazy and shot off every M-16 round he had—hundreds of them. He threw probably 100 or 150 hand grenades. He shot a hundred or so M-69 grenade launchers, and he fired off four or five claymore mines. This guy was crazy, and the other guys who were pulling bunker guard with us got scared and ran up the hill while he was still shooting and throwing hand grenades. The people there were ready to blow him away because they didn't know what on earth he was doing; they knew he had a tremendous amount of ammunition down there, but they also knew I was still down there, so they couldn't do anything. The uncanny part is that I slept through the whole thing while this guy just went totally crazy, but God protected me through the whole ordeal. "For He will give His angels charge concerning you, to guard you in all your ways" (Ps. 91:11).

Probably the one incident that made the greatest impact on me, twenty years after the fact, was the time when the chaplain and I went out to a LZ right on the Laotian border. It was a temporary fire support base with probably no more than fifty people maximum on this little hill, and they had put some mortars and some artillery there to support the troops that were down in the valley fighting. During a service the chaplain was holding, there were dozens of mortar rounds that began to hit directly within the perimeters of this very small building where we were located. In fact, we took a number of direct mortar hits as the hill was in the process of being assaulted. I had my M-16 out. I didn't use it, but we were close enough I could actually see the fire from the muzzles of the Vietnamese weapons. Because the chaplain wasn't expendable, they sent a chopper. They wanted to get him out of there, and I was told to go with him. Within an hour of the time we left, that whole place was overrun. I honestly didn't think much about it at the time because it was just another day in Vietnam, but several years later something happened letting me know how supernaturally God had intervened. I was in Chicago, and a man gave me a book in which he and eleven other people had described their Vietnam experience. His testimony was really powerful, so I started reading the others and discovered three of them were there at the exact time I was. Two of them were from my division, and one of the stories was telling about a battle fought on a fire support base right on the Laotian border, and he was one of the very few people who lived through this particular ordeal. I realized he had to have been talking about the exact same battle where I was. The thing that impacted me so much was that he wrote it from an unbeliever's perspective. At the time he wrote it he wasn't born again, and he described *the terror* that engulfed him. When I was there I loved God with all of my heart, so I was fine if the Lord was ready to take me home—not because I was discouraged with the war, but because I was so in love with the Lord I was ready to meet Him at any time. Therefore, when we were in that situation, and it looked as though we were going to be overrun and every person killed, instead of fear, I was feeling the peace of God and excitement that today could be the day I am going to see my Lord.

I remember watching the fire coming from their weapons and feeling nothing at the time except a love for those poor, lost souls who were headed for hell. It was like I had a bubble around me, and I never experienced fear because my heart was so filled with peace. But twenty years after the war, as I read that testimony of what I believe to be the same battle I was involved in, I had a flashback. *And I saw through the eyes of an unbeliever what it was like to go through that conflict without being in relationship with God.* So twenty years after being out of Vietnam, I had panic and terror hit me so hard it took me months to deal with it and get over the fear. God opened a curtain and let me see how it would have been had I not known Him intimately. I thank God for His *shield* that protects us mentally and emotionally, as well as physically. "He who dwells in the shelter of the Most High will abide in the shadow of the Almighty" (Ps. 91:1). "Because he [Andrew] has loved Me, therefore I will deliver him; I will set him securely on high, because he has known My name" (v. 14).

After that experience I realized what an advantage I had while I was in Vietnam. I was truly seated together with Him, watching the war from a much higher perspective—in His shelter where there is no fear. I thank God I *knew* Him. I shudder to think what it must have been like for those who were fighting with me who didn't know God in an intimate way. Truly, He has never left me nor forsaken me (Heb. 13:5).

Author's Note: For more than three decades, Andrew Wommack has traveled America and the world teaching the truth of the gospel. For more information about Andrew Wommack's ministry, contact him at 719.635.1111 or www.awmi.net.

AL CASTRO

Al Castro: On Right

My name is Al Castro, and I'm from New York City. I was sworn in as a patrolman in the New York Police Department, and I hold the rank of sergeant. I'm also the police firearms instructor of former law enforcement. On May 21, after returning from the police memorial in Washington DC, I was approaching New York City in the Bronx area, going toward building 33 from the parking lot when someone shot me with a pellet rifle on the side of my collarbone. The impact threw me up against the wall. A construction canopy allowed me to take cover and prevent any other shots to the face or to the body. At that point I called 911 for backup. EMS responded, and the inspector from the 205th precinct also responded, and I was transported to Covey Hospital for evaluation. Blood samples were taken, and I started receiving letters. I assumed they were doctor bills, but it was a letter concerning the results of the blood test.

I received a certified letter telling me to bring a family member and come in to that office. At that point, I felt it must be bad news. As soon as I came to the doctor's office, they did a sonogram, which showed that I had a cancer mass the size of a fifty-cent piece. The doctor sat down with me and informed me that I had very little time to live, and then he just walked out of the office. At that point I started pacing back and forth and praying that somehow there had been a mistake. I was thinking that perhaps I needed other medical evaluation before going with what that one doctor determined. After he came back, I just said, "God bless you; have a great day," and I left. I kept my cell phone off and drove up to Westchester County as I listened to worship music. Tears started welling up in my eyes as the Holy Spirit began working on me.

That shot was actually a real blessing since I would not have known about the cancer and, more than likely, when I found out, it would have been too late. The following day they gave me another appointment. I spoke to the female doctor, and she said, "I'm going to schedule you for a CAT scan and an MRI. Then I'm going to schedule you to see a specialist." I mentioned that the doctor had said that I had very little time to live, and she told me, "He had no right to tell you that. Only the Man above makes that decision. And he does not have a direct connection with the Man above."

They scheduled me for the CAT scan and the MRI. Then I went in to the specialist. It was a liver specialist, because the cancer mass was actually forming around the liver. I saw the doctor, and he said, "We're planning to hit you with Trace, which is another form of chemo." So I was scheduled to go on October 27 to the doctor for the Trace treatment in the main artery. When they set me up so they could put the catheter in my main artery in the lower level, they said to me, "We're going to give you something for the pain, because it's going to be very painful."

I said, "No, I don't want anything for the pain. I wanna be up until that area where you're going to puncture and put the catheter in is taken care of." To be honest with you, I wanted to be praying on it. As I was lying on the table, I had my hands open. I looked around, and there were three different booths with cameras and doctors evaluating what was going on. At that point I just started praying. I started seeing flashes of light, and I kept saying to myself, "Lord, help me get out of this. I've served You in so many different ways. You know I'll be there whenever I'm called upon to serve You. Just give me one more chance and get me out of this."

They kept pulling the camera in with the catheter. At that point I asked the medical staff, "Is it almost over?" and they said to me, "We haven't started yet."

"You've gotta be kidding me. It has already been going on for three hours!" I just kept praying. Finally, after four hours the treatment was over, and they laid me down in the stretcher. The doctor warned me, "You cannot move for another nine hours or you'll bleed internally."

At that point they took me to have a CAT scan, and the X-ray tech said, "You look like a big guy, so just pull yourself up on this metal bar."

I said, "I need to speak to your supervisor. My understanding is that the chief surgeon told me that I could not move; otherwise, I would bleed internally. If you consider me as a person who's just been shot or stabbed, you'd have to try to find another way to position me to take the CAT scan." At that point they did the CAT scan and admitted to me that I was right, based on the information that they also got from the surgeon—that I was not supposed to move for another nine hours, otherwise I'd bleed internally.

As they transported me upstairs to my room, I met with the doctor in charge of the amount of chemo I was supposed to be receiving, and he said, "It is amazing that we went in, and we didn't see anything at all but a shadow. We didn't see anything at all, but a shadow! You're going to have a lot of side effects from the chemo—vomiting, body aches, chills. There's going to be a nurse coming by every half hour for an hour and a half. They will supply you with medication for the pain."

As the nurses came by, I told them I was fine. I was not feeling any chills, any pains or body aches. The next day they evaluated me, and late that afternoon they released me, and I went home. On my way out, I just went straight to the church so all the brothers and sisters in Christ saw just a glow in my face. I wasn't supposed to be walking any stairs, but I was able to make it to the top step of the church and enter the church. I just knelt down and thanked the Lord for the miracle He brought about in my life. I continue to tell myself and all the brothers in Christ how wonderful the Lord works. Psalm 91 is such a faithful covenant.

The following day, I went to see my doctors, and they said, "It's amazing! When we entered, all that was there was blood. We're going to keep doing the MRI just to evaluate everything. Then after a while we'll shoot the MRI every six months instead of every three months just to keep an eye on things." Since then, the Lord has taken me out of that pit and really placed me in a position to serve Him in so many different ways. Ever since then I've been very involved with the youth ministry, reaching out to other police officers, firefighters, and so forth. It's been a blessing. I just really want to take the opportunity to praise the Lord for the miracle He's caused in my life.

Castro, on far left, stands with other law enforcement officers.

I am currently the president of the New York Regional Police, N.Y.S. 636 F.O.P. and I am also a member of an executive board as a state trustee with the New York State Fraternal Order of Police. The Fraternal Order of Police has become the largest professional police organization in the country. They are proud professionals working on behalf of law enforcement officers from all ranks and levels of government.

Al Castro on left

MIKE DISANZA

Mike DiSanza, NYPD
President and Founding Officer of *Cops for Christ* International

Author's Note: Mike gave us this testimony in his own words. His story gave me chills when I heard him telling it in his strong New York accent. Through his story I was moved by Mike's humor, but I could feel the undercurrent of urgency in him. Mike gave me one clear message to get out: "Too much of our time is spent worrying about things that don't matter, like our green lawn having a brown spot! If we don't get the gospel out, people are going to hell. One day we will wake up in forever. And it is a forever hell." Mike shared over the phone the dramatic testimony of his unusual introduction to Christ and his wife's reluctant conversion. I would encourage you to get his book and share it with a friend, because his testimony was every bit as dramatic as the Psalm 91 story of protection. Here's Mike's story in his own words.

Over my system came the message "Seventy-second Street and Broadway, Manhattan!" I knew the meaning of the code: cop in trouble and needs assistance. I rushed to the subway where there was a crowd of people around the cop, and they refused to let him get his prisoner. I walked directly over and cuffed the prisoner. The crowd went wild.

One man shouted, "Here comes the train! Let's throw the cop in the subway!" The crowd converted into a mob. I felt myself moving toward the subway track, being pushed by this angry crowd who was intending to hurl me onto the tracks in front of the speeding train. I could hear the sound and see the lights of the oncoming train coming out from the tunnel. I was being pushed toward the pit.

Being a new Christian, I cried out the best prayer I knew, "Jesus, help!" Suddenly two big black guys got up and started pushing the crowd. They parted the crowd and got over to me and said, "Follow us!" I grabbed the prisoner and followed as they parted the mob, and I felt the other cop right on my heels hanging on to my jacket. The two men ushered us back to the patrol car, and I loaded the prisoner in the backseat. He was still screaming his mouth off about how he hated cops. I turned around to thank the two strangers and was surprised that neither of them was there. "Oh, well," I thought, and muttered my thanks to them anyway.

I jumped in, and the other cop got in next to the driver. He thanked me gratefully for my help. I deflected the compliment and said to him, "Thank God for those two big black guys pushing the crowd apart, telling us to follow them and moving us to the car!"

He said, "I didn't hear nothing! I didn't see nothing!" He continued, "And I never heard anyone tell us to follow them!"

Still puzzled, I asked, "Eddie, how could you NOT see them? You were right behind us!"

When I turned around, I read this message in 3-D through the windshield: *Angels are ministering spirits to help those who will believe* . . . (See Hebrews 1:14.) It was at that moment I realized what had happened and said to myself, "My gosh, those guys were angels!" God really does give His angels charge concerning us (Ps. 91:11)!

Order Mike's book, *A Cop for Christ*, at 3231 S. Eagle Point, Inverness, FL 34450 or at www.acopforchrist.com.

JOHN JOHNSON

John Johnson
Texas Youth Commission
Special Tactics and Response Team

As a former leader of the Special Tactics and Response (STAR) team at our local Texas Youth Commission juvenile correctional facility, I was at times called upon to travel across the state to other facilities that were having problems. Our duty was to restore and maintain safe operations in facilities that were struggling. This is usually a risky adventure since we are required to control violent behavior of incarcerated juveniles without the use of guns. Tension is usually high between staff and the youth we are charged to control.

Before I started going on these trips, I had been learning from Peggy Joyce Ruth's *Psalm 91* books about the special covenant of protection God provides. God's Word works, and I learned to apply these biblical truths to my work assignments. I knew the risks going into these tense situations, and I prepared my response teams through physical training, proper equipping, and, most importantly, by praying His protection over me and each of my team members.

Each time we traveled, God blessed each of my team members

and me by protecting us physically and in every other way. At each facility where we were sent, we were always outnumbered by the youth. However, every time, just like Psalm 91 says, they would fall at our side.

One incident in particular stands out. I regularly would train our STAR team to control riot situations. On this particular trip, we definitely had to put this training to work. One dorm of youth overpowered staff and took control of the unit, tearing it up severely. The guys went crazy and ripped a water fountain from the wall, completely destroyed the washer and dryer, and threw a TV through a glass window. It was not a pretty sight. We were charged to take it back, and we went in quoting Scripture and fighting the battle spiritually. It took less than sixty minutes. We faced heavy objects being thrown at us and other dangerous, homemade weapons that had been fashioned to harm us. We were not afraid of any of those arrows flying against us. Some of the youth were injured—but not one staff member was hurt. Let me repeat that—not one staff member was hurt! I had prayed this psalm of protection over us, and, praise God, we were able to take control of the unit without being harmed. I was determined not to let the enemy hurt my staff or let him cause any more destruction now that Jesus was in the house, but I am still amazed as I think of what God did for us. It felt like His shield went before us, and I came out with not even one scratch or bruise! After peace had been restored, we walked through the dorm, and I recovered a twelve-inch-long homemade knife of razor-sharp, one-half-inch-thick glass taken from a shattered television, among other dangerous objects. These weapons could have easily killed one of our staff. With God's protection, that did not (and could not) happen.

Our superintendent, a godly man of faith, would also send us out under a covering of prayer. Every time, we brought home every man and woman from our team, safe and sound. God not only protected us, but He also honored our efforts. Based on our actions to provide STAR team help to our sister facilities in need, my STAR team earned the 2005 Institutional Team award from the TYC Executive Director. We cheated, however, by using an extra piece of gear—our Psalm 91 shield.

JEFF AND MELISSA PHILLIPS: MIRACLE IN IRAQ
by Crystal Phillips

Crystal Phillips has a master's degree in clinical Christian counseling. She is ordained in the ministry of counseling and is a licensed pastoral counselor with the National Christian Counselor Association, as well as a licensed chemical dependency counselor in the state of Texas.

Every mom dreads that phone call or letter that comes with news to devastate the rest of her life. A verse every parent needs to memorize is Psalm 112:7: "He will not fear evil tidings; his heart is steadfast, trusting in the LORD." Many times as I head toward a ringing phone in the dead of the night, I am praying this verse, "I will not fear a report of evil tidings because I am trusting in Your promises, Lord," before I ever pick up the receiver.

Most of us are not sure how we will react to an evil report, but I have found that faith grounded in the Word of God never fails. On January 17, 2003, I stood at San Diego Harbor watching my son, Jeff, a corporal in the United States Marine Corps, board the USS *Bonhomme Richard*, one of the seven warships heading for Iraq. My daughter-in-law and I were among thousands of family members treading water in a sea of emotions as we said good-bye to our loved ones. As we stood in the shadows of those gigantic ships, the feelings were ominous and foreboding.

Being told that my son could not take personal belongings on this trip, including his Bible, concerned me. I believe the Word of God is the only thing you should never leave at home. I felt somewhat eased by the fact that Jeff had a good foundation in the Word, and I was sure that the Holy Spirit would bring scriptures to his mind in times of need. Still, I felt that I had to *stock his arsenal* by giving him something that he could get his hands on fast. I had a book titled *God's Promises* in my suitcase, and the night before he shipped out I went through it and underlined specific verses, but that didn't seem to be quite enough. Knowing Psalm 91 and declaring those promises over my children for years inspired me to write out the verses inside the front cover (inserting Jeff's name throughout). I then slipped the book inside his seabag.

Days turned to weeks before we received mail from our son. His letters spoke of gratitude for the book, tremendous faith, direction, and encouragement for us to stay strong, followed by comments about the peace and assurance he was receiving from the Word.

About a week before President Bush declared war and we were all awakened to *Shock and Awe*, a local reporter asked if he could interview me. He was writing a story to be featured in the local newspaper, covering the thoughts and feelings of families with loved ones going to war. I spoke repeatedly of my faith in God and His promises of protection. Soon after war was declared, national television brought some of the horror into our living rooms, and we, along with most of the world, watched and waited. Soon afterward the reporter called and asked me if I still felt strong in my faith after hearing that there had been American casualties. I told him *yes* and mentioned Psalm 91. He asked me what it was about those particular verses that gave me faith. I proceeded to read him the entire contents of Psalm 91.

Seven days following the declaration of war, my husband and I received a large brown envelope in the mail from the state senator's office. The address on the envelope was handwritten to us. Inside was a letter signed and stamped with the senator's official seal. It was a letter bearing an evil report, offering condolences for the loss of our son.

Scanning over the first few lines brought me to a *crisis of belief.* Knowing that I am not a particularly strong person in my own strength, I look back now and find that I am quite amazed at the way I responded. Without God and the assurance of His promises, I know that I would have crumbled. My first response was, "This is a mistake, and *I will not believe* this evil report!" I at first thought that I would ignore it and throw the letter away. Then I realized that I had to continue to declare God's promises that are written in Psalm 91. The Word of God tells us in 2 Corinthians 10:5 that the battle is in our thought life. I became more adamant about declaring God's Word, and I refused to fall for the enemy's trap. Then I thought, "I have to call the senator's office to let them know about this mistake so other errors like this will be avoided." Making that call led to a long wait for a response, but I refused to spread the evil report. My daughter-in-law called, but I didn't tell her. I didn't even call my husband. For approximately two hours I paced through my house, vocally fighting a spiritual battle by loudly declaring the promises of God's Word. Some may disagree, not seeing the urgency of such action, but I knew that I had to line my thoughts, my confessions, and my agreement up with God's Word. I knew that my son's life was on the line! The devil had devised a plan to take my son's life, and I had no choice but to stand in the gap. I could not agree with the *evil report.* The letter was a tool to attempt to cause me to give up my confession of faith so the enemy could gain the access that he desired.

The blood of Jesus and the miraculous power and protection of God, which are unlimited by time or distance, are what placed my son under the shadow of His almighty wings. I would not give the enemy entry! Doubters might ask if I believe that the outcome could have been different. My answer to that is a definite *YES!* My son was in and out of foxholes, dodging rounds of fire that were falling inches from his feet. Had I placed my agreement with the enemy and lost my will to trust, pray, declare, and believe God, my son might not be here today.

Finally the phone rang with a profuse apology and confirmation that the letter had been sent by mistake. At that point, I called and shared the experience with my husband, assuring him that "all is well." Still months passed before we heard the voice of our son. I could never adequately describe how wonderful it was on that Thursday in June, around 2:00 a.m. in the morning, when we heard Jeff say, "What's up? I'm in Germany waiting to fly to California. Can you book me a flight to Dallas on Friday night, and will you pick me up?"

That weekend I told my two sons and their wives about the letter and brought it out for them to see. Each of them felt a sense of trauma after reading the letter. My two daughters-in-law and my older son, David, all said they didn't think they would have been able to handle hearing about the letter before Jeff's return. Each member of our family knows that without God's miraculous intervention, the enemy would have won. We all experienced a renewed growth in faith and trust in the promises and protection of God's Word, and we will always proclaim the truth and faithful delivery of Psalm 91.

Envelope containing letter from Senator Troy Fraser, addressed to
Mr. and Mrs. David Phillips

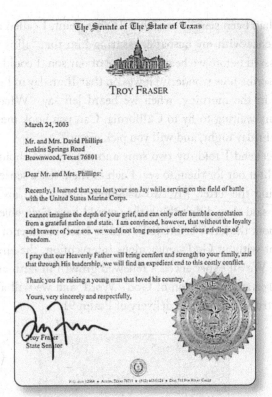

The Senate of The State of Texas

TROY FRASER

March 24, 2003

Mr. and Mrs. David Phillips
Jenkins Springs Road
Brownwood, Texas 76801

Dear Mr. and Mrs. Phillips:

Recently, I learned that you lost your son Jay while serving on the field of battle with the United States Marine Corps.

I cannot imagine the depth of your grief, and can only offer humble consolation from a grateful nation and state. I am convinced, however, that without the loyalty and bravery of your son, we would not long preserve the precious privilege of freedom.

I pray that our Heavenly Father will bring comfort and strength to your family, and that through His leadership, we will find an expedient end to this costly conflict.

Thank you for raising a young man that loved his country.

Yours, very sincerely and respectfully,

Troy Fraser
State Senator

P.O. Box 12068 • Austin, Texas 78711 • (512) 463-0124 • Dial 711 For Relay Calls

Letter of condolence from Senator Troy Fraser to Mr. and Mrs. David Phillips

CAPTAIN NICK CATECHIS: ARMY TRANSPORT UNIT MIRACLE, IRAQ

by Kay Gibson
Cofounder, Houston Marine Moms

About a year ago I met this *army mom*, Judith Cook, who was helping her son's unit—the 15th Transportation Unit from Fort Sill, Oklahoma, get ready to deploy to Iraq three days after Christmas 2004. Judith's son Nick is a captain of the Army Transport Unit, with 150 soldiers in this unit. The commander's wife contacted Judith and told her this group delivers supplies on the road between the Baghdad Airport and Abu Ghraib; therefore, they were expecting extremely high casualties. She was wondering if Judith would start making a quilted banner with a gold star in memory of each soldier they expected to be killed in action or severely injured. Judith asked what sort of casualty rate they were expecting. She was told 50–75 percent! On the Internet, Judith found some camouflage bandanas with the Ninety-first Psalm printed on them. The Ninety-first Psalm is considered the *psalm of protection* for our troops. Judith hand-delivered these bandanas to the soldiers in this unit and *made them promise to say this psalm every day before their missions.* Every day both the officers and soldiers would say this psalm together.

During the deployment Nick's unit was attacked on an almost-daily

basis with IEDs and mortars, as well as snipers. There were countless stories of mortars that never detonated, mortars that exploded
nearby, but no shrapnel injuries to Nick's group, no ambushes on their
Humvees, and no injuries. I have a picture of a bullet hole through the
window of Nick's Humvee. It missed him, his driver, and the mortar
man by an inch.

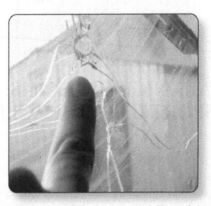

"Bullet hole that missed my son's head, his gunner's legs and the driver's head."
(submitted by Judith Cook)

In another incident, several of Nick's men were in the mess hall when
a mortar exploded less than twenty feet away. Shrapnel was all around,
yet none of the soldiers were injured. There was an attack on the army
buildings where the soldiers sleep, and three of the buildings were damaged, but the mortar that landed on top of Nick's building was a dud.
Several of Nick's men were in a PX near Baghdad when it was attacked.
Everyone in the PX was injured—except Nick's men. I received the following e-mail from Nick:

> We got hit again really bad night before last in three separate
> engagements. We received small arms fire on the first two, and
> another explosive on the third. I've attached a photo of the
> vehicle that took most of the blast. Remarkably, other than a
> possible concussion and some ringing ears, no one was hurt

seriously. This armor we have is really good stuff. Unfortunately we've had the chance to try it out on more than one occasion, but at least we know it is good stuff. We had a mortar attack also on the same day. One of the guys was outside working and heard a really loud noise and had rocks thrown on him. He looked over and saw an unexploded mortar lying on the gravel about 8–10 feet from him. Needless to say, he took off running. *If you are praying for us, it must be working. That's the only explanation of how no one has been seriously injured yet.*
—NICK 7-23-05

Day after day these soldiers gathered to pray this psalm together. In December 2005, after almost a year in Iraq, Nick and his unit returned home—all 150 soldiers. They did not lose ONE soldier, nor were any of them injured! THE POWER OF PRAYER IS AWESOME!

Oliver North and Chaplain Hester

PAM WRIGHT AND GENERAL PETRAEUS

I just got back with my oldest daughter from attending my son's graduation at Fort Benning, Georgia, from Ranger School. It was a powerful and moving experience, and we had an unexpected surprise! The guest speaker at the graduation ceremony turned out to be General David Petraeus, who just happened to be at Fort Benning visiting his son who is in airborne school, before he went on to Washington to testify before Congress. I had the tremendous privilege of meeting him and was able to give him a copy of your book, which he graciously received, and he asked me to continue to pray for our troops. I am praying the Lord's purposes will be fulfilled through this unexpected contact!

IN HIS LOVE,
PAM WRIGHT
FT. BENNING, GA

A PRAYER COVENANT

PERSONAL PSALM 91 COVENANT

Copy and enlarge this Psalm 91 covenant prayer to pray over yourself or your loved one—inserting his or her name in blanks.

_____ dwells in the shelter of the Most High and he/she _____ abides in the shadow of the Almighty. _____ says to the Lord, "My refuge and my fortress, my God, in whom I trust!" For it is God who delivers _____ from the snare of the trapper and from the deadly pestilence [fatal, infectious disease]. God will cover _____ with His pinions, and under His wings _____ may seek refuge; God's faithfulness is a shield and bulwark.

_____ will not be afraid of the terror by night, or of the arrow that flies by day; of the pestilence that stalks in darkness, or of the destruction that lays waste at noon. A thousand may fall at _____'s side, and ten thousand at his/her right hand; but it shall not approach _____. _____ will only look on with his/her eyes, and see the recompense of the wicked. For _____ has made the Lord his/her refuge, even the Most High, _____'s dwelling place. No evil will befall _____, nor will any plague come near _____'s tent. For He will give His angels charge concerning _____ to guard _____ in all his/her ways. They will bear _____ up in their hands, lest _____ strike his/her foot against a stone. _____ will tread upon the lion and cobra, the young lion and the serpent he/she will trample down. "Because _____ has loved Me," [God said], "therefore I will deliver him/her; I will set _____ securely on high, because _____ has known My name. _____ will call on Me, and I will answer _____. I will be with _____ in trouble; I will rescue _____ and honor _____. With a long life I will satisfy _____, and let him/her behold My salvation."

NOTES

FOREWORD

1. H.A. de Weerd, ed., *Selected Speeches and Statements of General of the Army George C. Marshall* (Washington DC: The Infantry Journal, 1945), quoted in Carl Joachim Hambro, "The Nobel Peace Prize 1953 Presentation Speech," December 10, 1953, http://nobelprize.org/nobel_prizes/peace/laureates/1953/press.html#not_8 (accessed March 5, 2010).

2. Carey H. Cash, *A Table in the Presence* (Nashville, TN: Thomas Nelson, 2004), 217.

THE POWER OF PSALM 91

1. Walter B. Knight, *Knight's Master Book of 4,000 Illustrations* (Grand Rapids, MI: William B. Eerdman's Publishing Company, 1981), 526.

2—WHAT IS COMING OUT OF MY MOUTH?

1. Katherine Pollard Carter, *The Mighty Hand of God* (Kirkwood, MO: Impact Christian Books, 1992), 29–30.

2. Jackie Mize, *Supernatural Childbirth* (Tulsa, OK: Harrison House, 1993).

3—TWO-WAY DELIVERANCE

1. Joseph H. Friend and David B. Guralnik, eds., *Webster's New World Dictionary* (New York: The World Publishing Co., 1953), s.v. "pestilence."

5—A MIGHTY FORTRESS IS MY GOD

1. Herbert Lockyer, ed., *Nelson's Illustrated Bible Dictionary* (Nashville, TN: Thomas Nelson, Inc., 1995), s.v. "bulwark."

2. Friend and Guralnik, *Webster's New World Dictionary*, s.v. "bulwark."

3. Carter, *The Mighty Hand of God*, 31–32.

4. Ibid., 29–30.

8—I Will Not Be Afraid of the Pestilence

1. James Strong, *Strong's Exhaustive Concordance of the Bible* (Madison, NJ: Abingdon Press, 1974), s.v. "*pino*."

2. Friend and Guralnik, *Webster's New World College Dictionary*, s.v. "imbibe."

11—No Plague Comes Near My Family

1. Old English proverb.

12—Angels Are Watching Over Me

1. Cash, *A Table in the Presence*, 208.

2. C. S. Lewis, "Miracles," in *God in the Dock* (Grand Rapids, MI: William B. Eerdman's Publishers, 1970), 27–28.

3. Alan S. Coulson and Michael E. Hanlon, "The Case of the Elusive Angel of Mons," Legends and Traditions of the Great War, http://www .worldwar1.com/heritage/angel.htm (accessed March 16, 2010).

13—The Enemy Is Under My Feet

1. Strong, *Strong's Exhaustive Concordance of the Bible*, s.v. "dragon."

17—God Answers My Call

1. Joe Kissell, "The Battle of Dunkirk," Interesting Thing of the Day, http://itotd.com/articles/436/the-battle-of-dunkirk (accessed March 17, 2010).

20—God Satisfies Me With Long Life

1. Knight, *Knight's Master Book of 4,000 Illustrations*, 528. Reprinted by permission of the publisher; all rights reserved.

Section II—Testimonies

1. For more of the story, see *Refined by Fire* by Brian and Mel Birdwell, with Ginger Kolbaba (Tyndale, 2004). You can also visit www.facethefire .org for more information on Face the Fire Ministries with Brian and Mel Birdwell.

PEGGY JOYCE RUTH

PEGGY JOYCE RUTH ENJOYS challenging people to move into a deeper understanding of the Word of God. While working alongside her husband, Jack, who was a pastor in Brownwood, Texas, for thirty years, she has accumulated many exciting experiences. Peggy Joyce taught the Wednesday night adult Bible study each week at their church during those years, and she still teaches a weekly *Better Living* radio Bible study on one of their two Christian radio stations in Brownwood. Some of her favorite experiences include teaching on a Caribbean Christian cruise ship, being elected as team cook for thirty-two Howard Payne University students on a mission trip into the *Tenderloin* area of San Francisco, and going with them again on a mission trip to the Philippines where she conducted a conference sponsored by twenty Filipino churches.

Peggy Joyce Ruth has authored six books and has appeared on numerous television stations for interviews. She is a popular speaker for conferences because of her warm storytelling techniques, her easy-to-understand style of communicating the Word of God, and her pleasing sense of humor. Peggy Joyce has spoken on several of the various military bases. Workbooks are also available for chaplains to take their soldiers through an in-depth study of Psalm 91.

For speaking engagements, Peggy Joyce can be contacted at: (325) 646-6894 or (325) 646-0623.

HEAR PEGGY JOYCE!

To listen to the audio message "Those Who Trust in the Lord Shall Not Be Disappointed," as well as other teachings, including "Psalm 91" and "Peggy Joyce's Testimony," please visit www.peggyjoyceruth.org. All of her teachings may be downloaded for your own personal use.

OTHER BOOKS AVAILABLE BY AUTHORS

Psalm 91: God's Shield of Protection

New expanded version of the military edition with more testimonies, including Psalm 91 stories from firemen, policemen, and prison guards. Published by Creation House, this book is ideal for anyone whose job is putting him in harm's way. The testimonies in this book will thrill your heart while they demonstrate the love of the Lord and the awesomeness of His power like never before. The examples in this book are for those in military or those who live around constant danger.

Psalm 91 Workbook

Make it meaningful, make it real, make it mine! This workbook is based on the work of Peggy Joyce Ruth's examination of Psalm 91 through her books *Psalm 91: God's Umbrella of Protection* and *Psalm 91: God's Shield of Protection* (military). It is divided into fifteen lessons. Each lesson includes applicable parables or analogies to help you think through various life events, questions to initiate personal response to these concepts, fill-in-the-blank questions, and projects to work on as a group or as an individual.

Psalm 91 for Youth

Help your young person overcome his greatest fears! Would you like for your child to know how to overcome the fears that face him?

Psalm 91 for Youth uses the same format as *Psalm 91: God's Umbrella of Protection*, with a similar verse-by-verse look at God's covenant of protection, but it is written on a reading level for youth and filled to overflowing with testimonies, illustrations, a picture album, and application helps to make this truth come alive.

My Own Psalm 91 Book

Teach your child his covenant at an early age! *My Own Psalm 91 Book* will help your preschooler get these important concepts in his heart at an early age. Thirteen hardback pages of illustrations and a paraphrased look at Psalm 91 by Peggy Joyce will keep even your youngest child wanting you to read to him from his very own copy! Available in English, Spanish/English, Korean/English, Chinese Traditional/English, and Portuguese/English (with other languages soon available).

Tormented: Eight Years and Back

Tormented: Eight Years and Back is the heartwarming story of a young woman's struggle through eight tormenting years of emotional illness, electrical shock treatments, prescription drugs, and hopelessness—culminating in absolute victory made possible only by God's supernatural delivering power. It is one of the most comprehensive books on protection from demonic forces that you will most likely ever read. Peggy Joyce Ruth tells you her personal testimony of God's delivering power and gives you scriptures to help you stay free!

Special: Add $2 for this teaching on CD.

God's Smuggler Jr. by Angelia Ruth Schum (Peggy Joyce Ruth's daughter)

This is the true story of someone who prayed for anything but an average life..."God, never let my life be boring!" You'll be amazed at how God answered that prayer. As the story develops in an exotic place, there is nonstop action with twists and turns as Bibles are smuggled past armed guards into communist lands. This book will challenge you to pray that same prayer without stipulations: "God, please don't ever let my life be boring!"

Is There a Yearning in Your Heart to Trust God More?

Those Who Trust the Lord Shall Not Be Disappointed is a comprehensive study on developing a TRUST that cannot be shaken. This book has the potential of building a trust in God like nothing you have ever read. Deep down, we direct our disappointments toward God—thinking that somehow He let us down. We trust God for our *eternal* life; why then can we not trust Him amid the adversities of *daily* life? Peggy Joyce Ruth has a unique way of showing that victorious living depends upon our unwavering trust in God. She demonstrates with scores of personal experiences just how faithful God really is and details how you can develop the kind of trust that will not disappoint. *Those who trust in the Lord shall not be disappointed.*

Special: Add $2 for this teaching on CD.

CPSIA information can be obtained
at www.ICGtesting.com
Printed in the USA
LVHW091952181122
733282LV00008B/207

9 781636 411873